Software Metrics

CHAPMAN & HALL COMPUTING SERIES

Computer Operating Series
For micros, minis and mainframes
2nd edition
David Barron

Microcomputer Graphics
Michael Batty

The Pick Operating System
Malcolm Bull

A Course of Programming in FORTRAN
3rd edition
V. J. Calderbank

Expert Systems
Principles and case studies
2nd edition
Edited by Richard Forsyth

Machine Learning
Principles and techniques
Edited by Richard Forsyth

Software Quality
Theory and management
Alan C. Gillies

Expert Systems
Knowledge, uncertainty and decision
Ian Graham and Peter Llewelyn Jones

Computer Graphics and Applications
Dennis Harris

Software Metrics
A practitioner's guide to improved product development
K.-H. Möller and D. J. Paulish

Artificial Intelligence and Human Learning
Intelligent computer-aided instruction
Edited by John Self

Formal Concepts in Artificial Intelligence
Fundamentals
Rajjan Shinghal

Techniques in Computational Learning
An introduction
C. J. Thornton

Artificial Intelligence
Principles and applications
Edited by Masoud Yazdani

ACCESS
The Pick enquiry language
Malcolm Bull

Techniques in ...

Artificial ...

Software Metrics

A practitioner's guide to improved product development

K.-H. Möller
Technical Director

and

D. J. Paulish
Task Leader
ESPRIT PYRAMID project
Siemens AG
Munich
Germany

IEEE COMPUTER SOCIETY PRESS

IEEE PRESS

CHAPMAN & HALL COMPUTING
London · Glasgow · New York · Tokyo · Melbourne · Madras

Published by Chapman & Hall, 2–6 Boundary Row, London SE1 8HN

Chapman & Hall, 2–6 Boundary Row, London SE1 8HN, UK

Blackie Academic & Professional, Wester Cleddens Road, Bishopbriggs, Glasgow G64 2NZ, UK

Chapman & Hall Japan, Thomson Publishing Japan, Hirakawacho Nemoto Building, 6F, 1–7–11 Hirakawa-cho, Chiyoda-ku, Tokyo 102, Japan

Chapman & Hall Australia, Thomas Nelson Australia, 102 Dodds Street, South Melbourne, Victoria 3205, Australia

Chapman & Hall India, R. Seshadri, 32 Second Main Road, CIT East, Madras 600 035, India

First edition 1993

Material in this book has been developed from work carried out by the PYRAMID research project, a collaborative research project funded by the European Commission under the ESPRIT II programme.

Printed in Great Britain by St Edmundsbury Press Ltd, Bury St Edmunds, Suffolk

ISBN 0 412 45900 0
ISBN 0 7803 0444 6 (IEEE Press, USA and Canada only)

Exclusive North American distribution rights assigned to
IEEE Press, 445 Hoes Lane, PO Box 1331, Piscataway, NJ 08855–1331
Order number PP0341-8
and
IEE Computer Society Press, 10662 Los Vaqueros Circle, PO Box 3014, Los Alamitos, CA 90720–1264
Order number 3035
This edition not for sale outside the USA and Canada

A catalogue record for this book is available from the British Library

Library of Congress Cataloging-in-Publication data available

∞ Printed on permanent acid-free text paper, manufactured in accordance with the proposed ANSI/NISO Z 39.48-199X and ANSI Z 39.48-1984

This book is dedicated to everyone who
has worked on a software project
that was behind schedule
or produced a product
that contained bugs

Contents

Acknowledgements

We are grateful to the PYRAMID Consortium and Siemens companies who have contributed their practices of software metrics, experience, and quality improvement techniques. We are fortunate both to have worked on the ESPRIT PYRAMID Project, whose purpose is to disseminate the positive experiences of quantitative approaches to software project management, and with an excellent team of European software experts. Specially the individuals within the PYRAMID Consortium who have contributed their ideas, feedback, criticism, and experience include Jean Jacques Lauture (Commission of the European Communities), Frédéric Copigneaux, Francis Escaffre (VERIDATAS), Anton Seigis, Helmut Neugebauer, Jürgen Berger (SIEMENS), Tom Ipoly, Phil Parsons (DATA LOGIC), Nabil Abu El Ata, Annie Drucbert (EUROEXPERT), Jim Hemsley, Phil Preedy, Eric Trodd (BRAMEUR), Catherine Dupont (CRIL), Yannis Kliafas (ATC), Roberto Lancellotti, Marco Maiocchi, Robert Cachia (ETNOTEAM), and Werner Phillipp, Ulrich Heitkötter, Herbert Schippers (RW–TÜV).

We wish to acknowledge the discussion, ideas, and feedback of the various SIEMENS company representatives; Bernd-Peter Settele, Wolfgang Heidrich, Ulrich-Heinz Heubach (Siemens Nixdorf Informations systeme), Gerd Wackerbarth, Siegfried Eder (Siemens Public Communication Networks), Ronald Vaupel, Eberhard Wildgrube (Siemens Private Communication Systems), and Steve Staats, Tom Bishop, Fred Geheb (Siemens Medical Electronics). We also wish to acknowledge the support given for this project by the SIEMENS AG Corporate Production and Logistics Department, particularly that given by Hermann Schmelzer and Bruno Freund.

Specific contributions were made to the book by the following individuals: Tom Ipoly (DATA LOGIC) – Software Quality Metrics Framework (Section 6.1), Frédéric Copigneaux (VERIDATAS) – Tools (Chapter 8) and with Serge Meurgues – Code Inspection Metrics (Chapter 12), Tom Ipoly, Phil Parsons, Noeleen Lowry, Lester Dudfield, Richard Francis, Mike Gilchrist (DATA LOGIC) – Best Practices (Chapter 10), Marco Maiocchi, Roberto Lancellotti, Adriana Bicego, Gualtiero Bazzana (ETNOTEAM) – Best Practices (Chapter 11), Ulrich Heitkötter (RW–TÜV) – Process Monitoring System Testing (Chapter 13), and Catherine Dupont (CRIL) – User Satisfaction Measurement (Chapter 14).

Finally, we would like to thank our families whose patience, support, and understanding were appreciated during the long hours necessary to complete this effort.

Preface

In many endeavors, numbers are used to characterize, compare, and record trends. In a managed enterprise, numbers are used to help control and improve performance in the pursuit of goals. Each number is a measurement of some process characteristic. 'If you can measure it, you can control it' may not be true of the weather, but it is true for most business processes.

The purpose of this book is to share successful experiences with applying software metrics to project management. It contains practical suggestions for implementing metrics. It also contains summaries of successful techniques on metrics implementation and the benefits that resulted within industrial organizations.

Many of the practices described were collected as part of the ESPRIT PYRAMID Project. The purpose of the PYRAMID Project is to collect and disseminate the best practical examples of metrics used to help manage real software projects on time, to budget, and with results that match customer expectations. The Project also encourages others to learn and gain from following the examples. The PYRAMID Project Consortium consists of nine companies from six countries who develop, test, and provide consulting services for software systems. The Consortium has access to the best practices of software metrics that are used in the world today.

This book contains a collection of suggestions concerning managing with metrics based upon techniques that have worked within industry. The suggestions must be tailored to the specific goals and develop process of the organization wishing to improve software product quality and develop team productivity. It is hoped that the application of these techniques on software metrics applied to project management will result in better higher quality products that are developed with more productive resources within a shorter time schedule.

1 Introduction

1.1 The Software Problem

Improving software product quality and performance and development team productivity has become a primary priority for almost every organization that relies on computers. While computer hardware performance has been doubling approximately every three years, improvements in software productivity have been increasing at a modest 4% annual rate (Jones, 1991; Putnam, 1991). As computers grow more powerful, the users demand more powerful, sophisticated software. The process of developing new software and maintaining old systems has in many cases been poorly implemented, resulting in large cost overruns and squandered business opportunities. The software problem is huge, affecting many companies and government organizations. According to recent studies, less than 1% of completed large software system projects are typically finished on time, within budget, and meet all user requirements. Furthermore, the average large software system project finishes over a year late and costs almost twice as much as the initial cost estimate. In the United Kingdom alone, it has been estimated that approximately one million pounds per hour of effort are wasted as a result of poor quality software.

The business press continually documents business failures that are attributable to problems involved with software development. Many senior executives and government officials are wondering why software development is so costly and takes so long. For example, a recent version of a popular personal computer spreadsheet application reached the market over a year behind schedule. It is estimated that this program was implemented in 400,000 lines of code, required 263 staff-years of effort, and cost $22 million, $15 million of which was invested in quality control testing activities. This is a relatively modest software project investment as compared to the software investment for implementing the US NASA Space Shuttle. This very large software system required 25.6 million lines of code, 22,096 staff-years of effort, and cost $1.2 billion (Schlender, 1989).

Substantial investment is being made for the development of new software and the maintenance and modification of existing software. The estimated code size and investment costs for some typical software product development applications are given in Table 1.1. Low development team productivity and poor product quality can result in lost business and reduced profitability within software business organizations (Figure 1.1).

Table 1.1 Typical SW Application Size and Investment

Product Application	*Size (MLOC)*	*Cost ($M)*
Operating System, Large Communication System	2-5	150-350
Mid-Sized Communication System	1-2	50-100
Data Base System, Compiler	0.4-1	9-22
Transaction Monitor	0.2-0.4	5-10
Monitoring System (Medical)	0.2-0.4	4-8

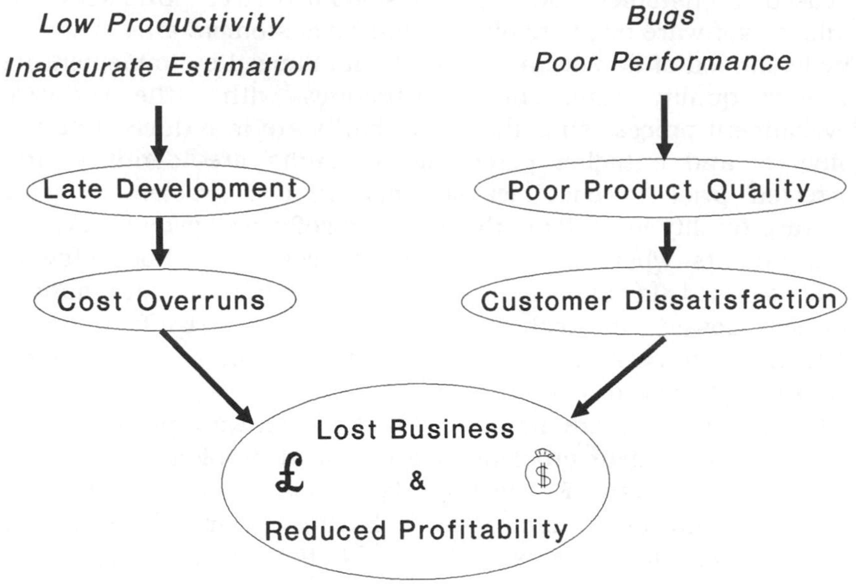

Figure 1.1 The Software Problem.

The large increasing demand for software and the modest improvement in software productivity is creating a major demand for skilled software engineers, managers, and quality specialists. It has been estimated that there are approximately 15 million software programmers worldwide. This demand is creating a general software engineering education lag and skills shortage.

One of the most frustrating aspects of today's software development problem for business executives is the large number of projects which are delivered to customers behind schedule. This results in missed sales opportunities and customer dissatisfaction. In many high technology businesses, the company that reaches the market first with a new product is the company that gains market share over its competitors. Thus, it is desirable to have the ability for accurate estimation of the development time for software products. It is also desirable to decrease the elapsed time from product conception to customer delivery.

Problems with software quality and performance can adversely affect the relations of a business with its customers. Software released to customers today is very seldom perfect. Undiscovered faults or software bugs are often found by customers after delivery. The likelihood of this occurring can be minimized by implementing software quality management techniques within the software development process such that fewer faults are introduced into the software, and a higher percentage of faults are identified and corrected prior to customer shipment. The problem of poor software quality is particularly acute for software systems used in environments where safety is a major concern. For software systems used in applications such as industrial automation, nuclear power, medical instrumentation, air traffic control systems, military systems, etc., a latent bug in the code could result in injury or loss of human life.

Many companies are discovering that the software problem is as much a management problem as a technical problem. Computer Science or Software Engineering is a relatively new technical discipline with programming work having a limited history of approximately forty years. Many of the good management practices and quality assurance techniques used in other engineering and production disciplines are also applicable to software development. Unfortunately, there are currently not enough software engineers trained in project and quality management. Conversely, relatively few business executives have experience with software engineering. This lack of knowledge may result in unrealistic business planning which fails to consider or underestimates the difficulty of developing and maintaining software products.

1.2 Measurement in Software Engineering

This book describes approaches for improving software quality and productivity by the application of quantitative methods or 'metrics'. The basis for this technique is the observation that you cannot easily manage what you cannot measure. A century ago, Lord Kelvin said, '... when you can measure what you are speaking about, and express it in numbers, you know something about it; when you cannot express it in numbers, your knowledge is of a meager and unsatisfactory kind; it may be the beginning of knowledge, but you have scarcely in your thoughts advanced to the stage of science ...'

The application of software metrics is a tool for effectively managing the software development and maintenance process.

Many metrics have been researched over the past fifteen years, but their application has been limited in practice. Within the past few years there has emerged a new wave of leading-edge software metrics' practitioners who have applied global metrics for the purpose of incrementally improving the software development process. Global metrics are indicators that relate to high-level size, product, and development process quality indicators that are of interest to the managers of a software development or maintenance activity. The aim of this book is to provide suggestions for the application of software metrics based upon practices that have been successfully used in industrial companies.

1.3 Approach

The approach for improving software quality, performance, and productivity using software metrics is straightforward. It begins with a documented software development process which will be incrementally improved over time. Goals are established with respect to the desired extent of quality and productivity improvements over a specified time period. These goals are derived from and are consistent with the strategic goals for the business enterprise.

Metrics are then defined that can be used to measure periodic progress in achieving the improvement goals. The metric data collected can be used as an indicator of development process problem areas, and improvement actions can be identified. These actions can be compared and analyzed with respect to the best return-on-investment for the business unit. The measurement data provides information for investing wisely in tools for quality and productivity improvement.

The metrics play a key role in setting up a closed-loop feedback mechanism within which incremental improvements can be made to the software development and maintenance process over time (Figure 1.2). These process improvements result in higher quality products and increased development team productivity, which in turn increases the competitiveness of the business enterprise.

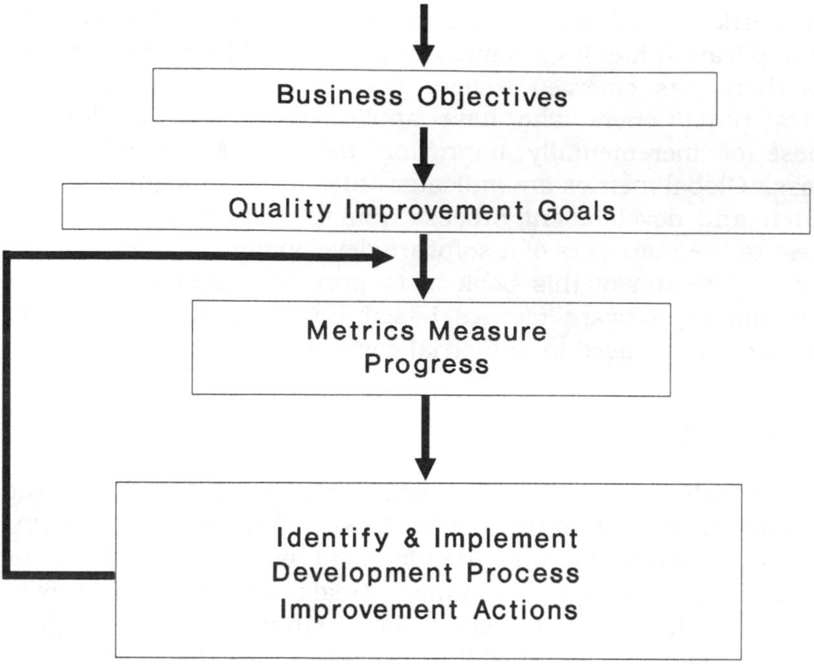

✓ *Use Metrics to Improve the Development Process*
✓ *'You Cannot Manage What You Cannot Measure'*

Figure 1.2 Software Metrics Approach.

The successful implementation of metrics is heavily dependent on the level of support provided by the business management of the company. Many of the benefits result from a positive change of development staff attitudes oriented towards improved quality. Management must actively support the Metrics Introduction Program in order to influence these corporate culture changes. The business goals must be clearly defined, and the Metrics Introduction Program goals should be supportive of these business goals.

1.4 Benefits

The implementation of a Metrics Introduction Program will result in many benefits for the business enterprise. These benefits will include lower development costs as a result of higher productivity, higher sales due to shorter development cycles, and improved customer satisfaction as a result of higher product quality. Lower costs and higher sales will result in increased profitability. The PYRAMID Consortium Partners have collectively observed quality improvements on the order of 35% per year. This is very much dependent on the starting point for improvement, and on the effectiveness of coupling the metrics data to actions designed to improve the software development process.

The use of metrics will improve the organization's ability to plan new projects. When historical project data is readily available, comparisons can be made between new projects and similar prior projects. This will improve the organization's ability to estimate costs and schedules for new projects such that better business decisions can be made concerning which projects should be funded and initiated.

The metric data should be made available to software project managers on a frequent basis, in a timely fashion in order to contribute to decision making. As a result, corrective actions can be made to the project plan to increase the probability of successful completion of the project. The metric data enables the project manager to measure the effects of his actions, and it helps him decide among technical and management alternatives. The metric data becomes a communication vehicle between business management and software product development, in order to evaluate the status of projects and the quality levels of products prior to shipment to customers.

The application of metrics should be beneficially used in conjunction with an overall corporate quality and productivity improvement program. This can be a key element in achieving a company culture in which high quality products and development process are valued.

A Metrics Introduction Program will result in an increase of customer confidence by demonstrating that a company has good knowledge of the strengths and weaknesses of its products and development process, and that it is taking positive actions to correct its weaknesses.

Metrication provides visibility on the entire software development process, and it thus reduces its apparent complexity.

This takes away some of the 'mystery' and 'wizardry' of software development, and makes it more understandable through its similarity to other industrial development processes.

It should be pointed out, however, that a Metrics Introduction Program by itself will not result in all these benefits. The Metrics Introduction Program is merely an aid for improving the software development process. The productive development of high quality products will depend on how well the process is implemented and managed. This will depend on many factors such as the quality and experience of the technical staff, the product/project complexity, the use of software tools, the required product reliability, the understanding of the application needs, the customer expectations, and other variables. It must be pointed out that the use of metrics is not a 'magic' solution by itself. It is, however, an important aspect in a holistic approach to the continuous pursuit of quality and productivity improvement, and achieving a corporate quality culture.

The Metrics Program and the related software development process improvement activities will in time become an integral part of the software project management culture. In time metrics will become an ongoing practice adopted and used by all project personnel.

1.5 Book Organization

This book contains both tutorial material oriented towards assisting practitioners of metrics, and summaries of best practices and resulting benefits of the application of metrics for a number of companies and projects in Europe and the United States. The suggestions that are given are based on techniques that have been previously applied in industry. The suggestions can be used to help establish a new Metrics Program, or improve an existing Program. It is hoped that the material in the book will encourage a more widespread application of quantitative approaches to software project management throughout industry.

The contents of the book are summarized below.

Chapter 1. ***Introduction.*** *This chapter introduces the subject of quantitative approaches to software project management using software metrics. A summary of the current problems associated with software project management is given. The software metrics approach and the anticipated resulting benefits are summarized.*

Chapter 2. ***Origins of Software Metrics.*** *This chapter summarizes the origins of software metrics. The key technology trends that were initiated in the 1970s that led to the use of quantitative approaches in the 1980s are indicated. It is projected that the use of software metrics for project management will become more widespread in the 1990s.*

Chapter 3. ***Software Quality and Productivity by Quantitative Methods.*** *This chapter identifies some of the uses of software metrics for improving software product quality and development team productivity.*

Chapter 4. ***Metrics Introduction Program Approach.*** *This chapter provides some practical suggestions concerning how to introduce and maintain a Metrics Program within an organization. It stresses the basic requirement for a documented software development process as a prerequisite and improvement opportunity coupled to the Metrics Program. The Seven-Step Metrics Introduction Program approach is described.*

Chapter 5. ***Common Implementation Problems.*** *This chapter describes some common implementation problems that can arise when metrics are applied within industrial organizations. The problems are described, and suggested actions are given to overcome the problems.*

Chapter 6. ***Metrics Characteristics.*** *This chapter discusses the general characteristics of useful metrics. The CSA Software Quality Metrics Framework is introduced. General guidance on the characteristics of good metrics is given for the purpose of selecting metrics that are most applicable to a specific corporate environment.*

Chapter 7. ***Example Metrics.*** *This chapter provides some example metrics which may be useful for establishing a Metrics Program. Examples of global metrics and phase metrics are given. Fault detection and prediction techniques are summarized. Relative performance values of metrics are discussed.*

Chapter 8. ***Tools.*** *This chapter provides guidance on the use of tools for supporting a Metrics Program. After an introduction which establishes the general lack of commercially available tools for metrics purposes, the remainder of this chapter gives guidance on the necessary desirable tool functions. Implementation of these functions is generally possible on commercially available spreadsheet, or data base packages.*

Chapter 9. ***Best Practices and Benefits Experience*** **-** ***Siemens.*** *This chapter describes some of the experiences of Siemens companies in Europe and the United States with applications of metrics. Information summarized includes an application overview, development process, metrics used, quality improvement techniques, and observed benefits. The practices used have been applied to both global and phase metrics.*

Chapter 10. ***Best Practices and Benefits Experience*** **-** ***Data Logic.*** *This chapter describes some of the experience of Data Logic with applying global metrics for improved software project management in the United Kingdom.*

Chapter 11. *Best Practices and Benefits Experience - ETNOTEAM.* *This chapter describes some of the experience of ETNOTEAM with applying metrics to their client companies through consulting projects in Italy.*

Chapter 12. *VERIDATAS Code Inspection Metrics.* *This chapter describes a VERIDATAS application of phase metrics to code inspections in France.*

Chapter 13. *RW-TÜV Process Monitoring System Testing.* *This chapter describes the experience of RW-TÜV in Germany with applying phase metrics to testing.*

Chapter 14. *CRIL User Satisfaction Measurement.* *This chapter describes the application by CRIL of subjective and phase metrics to the measurement of user satisfaction in France.*

Chapter 15. *Conclusions.* *This chapter summarizes the book emphasizing the benefits of a Metrics Program.*

Appendix A. *References.* *This appendix contains a bibliography on metrics documentation for the reader with further interest.*

Appendix B. *Glossary of Acronyms.* *This appendix contains a list of abbreviations used in the book.*

1.6 Conclusion

This book aims to document some of the best practices of software metrics that are currently used in industry. These best practices are incorporated into suggestions that are made for companies wishing to initiate a Metrics Introduction Program or improve an existing Metrics Program. In addition, the experience of a number of specific organizations is summarized. The best practices described in this book are summarized in Table 1.2. This experience summary includes information on the software development process, metrics, quality techniques used, and the benefits observed.

Table 1.2 Best Practices Summary

Company	*Practice Area*	*Application*
Siemens Nixdorf Informationssysteme	Quality Metrics	Computer System Software Development and Maintenance
Siemens Nixdorf Informationssysteme	Subjective Metrics	Custom Application Software
Siemens Medical Electronics	Metrics Program Introduction	Patient Monitoring System Product Development
Siemens Medical Electronics	Project Assessment	Small Sized Patient Monitor
Siemens Private Communication Systems	Global Metrics, Fault Prediction	Communication Systems
Siemens Automation	Metrics Program Introduction	Factory Automation Systems
Data Logic	Process Assessment by Metrics & Project Development Metrics	Customer Projects
Data Logic	Process Assessment by Metrics & Project Development Metrics	Customer Billing System
Data Logic	Global Metrics	Networked PCs
Data Logic	Global Metrics	Manufacturing

ETNOTEAM	Maintenance Product Assessment	Consulting
ETNOTEAM	Quality System Introduction	Banking
VERIDATAS	Code Review Metrics	Software Purchasing
RW-TÜV	Test Coverage Metrics	Safety Critical Process Monitoring System
CRIL	Customer Satisfaction Measurement	Transportation Company

After observing the software metrics practices of a large number of software development organizations, it can be concluded that the specific methods used are very diverse. For example, what may be considered as a good practice by a company in Germany could be a bad practice if used as is by a company in the United Kingdom. The practices described in this book in most cases must be tailored to the specific company, country, and quality culture of the environment in which they will be applied. This creates a difficulty for the metrics practitioner in that there is no simple formula which can be applied to increase quality and productivity. The best practices material in this book has been structured as chapters corresponding to the company of origin. In all cases the country of application has been identified. Table 1.3 classifies the organizations who have contributed best practices by the type of software quality problem to be solved. It can be concluded in all cases that the software development organizations described were successful in applying software metrics as a tool for improving their software development process. The improvements in their software development process resulted in higher quality products and more productive development teams.

Table 1.3 Problem to be Solved

SW Quality Problem	*Companies*
Large System SW Development	Siemens Nixdorf Informationssysteme, Data Logic
Application SW Development	Siemens Nixdorf Informationssysteme, Data Logic
Safety-Critical Systems Development	Siemens Medical Electronics, Siemens Automation, RW-TÜV
Large Communication System SW Development	Siemens Private Communication Systems
Embedded Real-Time System SW Development	Siemens Medical Electronics, Siemens Automation, RW-TÜV
Process Assessment	Siemens Medical Electronics, Data Logic, ETNOTEAM
Process Phase Improvement	VERIDATAS, RW-TÜV, CRIL
Introducing Metrics into an Organization	Siemens Medical Electronics, Siemens Automation, ETNOTEAM

2 Origins of Software Metrics

2.1 Primary Technology Trends

The application of software metrics has proven to be an effective technique for improving software quality and productivity. The best practices described in this book have been applied throughout the 1980s. Leading-edge practitioners such as those in the PYRAMID Consortium, as well as others in the United States and Japan, have created increasing interest in software metrics over the past few years.

The groundwork for the origins of the application of quantitative methods to software development was established in the 1970s (Coté, 1988). There were four primary technology trends which occurred at that time which have evolved into the metrics practices used today.

1. *Code Complexity Measures.* In the mid-1970s, there was significant research activity for developing measures of code complexity. These code metrics were easy to obtain since they could be calculated by automated means from the product code itself. Early examples of these techniques include McCabe's Cyclomatic Complexity Measure (McCabe, 1976) and Halstead's Software Science (Halstead, 1979).

2. *Software Project Cost Estimation.* These techniques were developed in the mid-1970s for estimating the effort and schedule that would be required to develop a software product, based upon an estimate of the number of lines of code necessary for implementation and other factors. Early examples of these techniques include Larry

Putnam's SLIM Model (Putnam, 1980) and Barry Boehm's COCOMO Model (Boehm, 1981).

3. *Software Quality Assurance.* The techniques of Software Quality Assurance were significantly improved during the late 1970s and early 1980s. Of particular interest to quantitative methods is the emphasis that was placed on the collection of fault data during the various phases of the software life-cycle (Möller, 1988).

4. *Software Development Process.* As software projects became larger and more complex, the need for a controlled software development process emerged. This process included defining the development life-cycle by finite sequential phases, and placing more emphasis on software project management with better control of resources (Basili, 1980). The measurement of resources and resulting development costs were collected using corporate cost accounting systems.

In the 1980s, these four software engineering technology trends provided the foundation and impetus for the improved management of software projects by quantitative methods (Figure 2.1). Leading-edge practitioners began applying metrics for the purpose of improving the software development process. One may compare this approach with the analogous situation of a factory production process in which statistical quality control measurements are used to manage and improve the production process. The application of metrics for improving the software development process was also consistent and complementary to many corporate quality improvement programs (e.g. Total Quality Management; Feigenbaum, 1983) which were implemented in the 1980s (Grady, 1987).

The analogy to a factory production process has been carried out in practice and name in the Japanese Software Factories, the earliest of which was established in 1969 as Hitachi Software Works (Cusumano, 1991). The Japanese Software Factories utilized metrics for analyzing the quality of the development process, and systematically improved their process over time. During the 1970s and 1980s software development within a limited number of organizations in Japan, Europe, and the United States evolved from a craft to a controlled development process which was continually improved. The use of metrics played a key role in improving the engineering knowledge and discipline of software development (Gill, 1991).

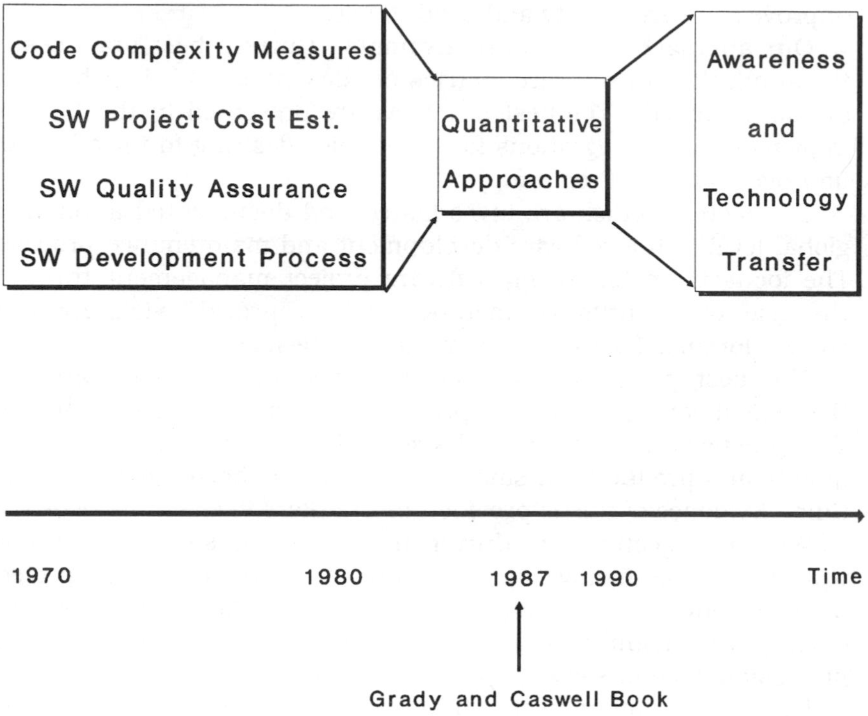

Figure 2.1 Origins of Software Metrics.

2.2 Metrics Today

Today's practices of software metrics utilize global indicators which provide insights into improving the software development and maintenance process. The improved process helps to achieve organizational goals established for improving software quality and development team productivity.

The primary technology diffusion message of this book is that the use of metrics can be a valuable aid in understanding the effect of actions that are implemented for improving the software development process. The metrics provide visibility and control for the complex software development process, and therefore they are valuable for providing guidance on improving the software development process, and for meeting organizational goals to improve software quality and productivity.

Our approach is to lead by example. Current best practices of the application of software metrics are described and their benefits are summarized. The best practices are presented in the form of implementation suggestions for companies desiring to introduce or improve a Metrics Program.

The metrics which are investigated and documented apply at a global level to the software development and maintenance process. The focus is on improving software project management through the use of quantitative methods, which provide visibility and control for all software development activities.

The best practices that are described in this book are not theoretical concepts, but are practices currently used in industry. The practices are known to have a positive impact on software quality and productivity, since their effect has been measured over time. Evidence of this is provided in Chapters 9-14 of this book.

We are projecting that during the 1990s the software industry will more commonly apply software metrics as a project management tool for improving software product quality and development team productivity. A general trend towards more professionalism in software project management is under way.

Larry Putnam projects that control offices will be more commonly established within companies in the 1990s for the purpose of measuring, planning, and controlling software projects (Putnam, 1991). These control offices will be centers of expertise for generating realistic plans for schedule, cost, and fault prediction. Their goal will be to improve software product quality and development team productivity by measuring and improving the software development process.

The widespread use of software metrics in the 1990s will be driven by executive or upper management's desire to create a more competitive software business. It has been observed that the limited number of companies that have applied quantitative approaches for improving the software development process have collectively reduced costs by 25% per year and shortened development schedules by nearly 10% per year (Putnam, 1991). These potential cost and schedule reductions will stimulate executive management's support of quantitative approaches to software project management as a strategic vehicle for achieving greater sales and profitability.

2.3 Metrics Use in the Future

We project that metrics use in the future will be applied more frequently for the prevention of faults within a feedback mechanism to analyze where problems have occurred so that the development process can be improved. Incorporating metrics into the activities associated with preventing faults will reduce the time delays from the point when a software development process improvement is implemented to when it positively impacts quality and productivity. This can be referred to as a 'Meta-Process' which is concerned with continual, rapid improvement at a global level to the software development process. This Meta-Process would include the mechanisms and procedures to predictively identify process improvements, monitor and track the actions for improvement, maintain the necessary training and documentation for newly introduced process improvements, and collect and maintain metrics data.

A current example of the use of metrics which will become more widely practiced in the future within a Meta-Process is a Software Defect Prevention Process (Mays, 1990). The Defect Prevention Process puts more emphasis on preventing defects from being injected during software product development rather than on defect detection through reviews and testing. This approach puts emphasis on collecting and analyzing defects to understand their cause, and views faults as an opportunity for improving the development process so as to prevent future faults. The Defect Prevention Process consists of four primary elements integrated into the software development process.

1. Causal Analysis meetings to identify root causes and suggest preventive actions.

2. Action teams which implement the preventive actions such as development process improvements.

3. Kickoff meetings for increasing awareness for

each phase of development.

4. Metrics collection, tracking, and distribution.

Another projection about metrics use in the future is based upon observation of organizations that have used metrics for an extended period of time such as Siemens Nixdorf Systems Software (Chapter 9). In these organizations, extensive historical metric data is available, and the development staff have substantial experience with metrics application within their specific environment. Over time the development activities exhibit a great deal of flexibility and informality. Metrics application for an organization with minimal experience becomes a training and communications vehicle which becomes ingrained within the organization over time. As the staff become more experienced there is less need for formal procedures and techniques. An analogy to the world of sport is when one lifts heavy weights over an extended period of time, overall strength level is incrementally increased.

3 Software Quality and Productivity by Quantitative Methods

3.1 Understanding Quality

This book provides suggestions based upon industrial experience for using software metrics for improving product quality and development team productivity. A basic understanding of quality and productivity tailored to the specific development environment is thus necessary in order for improvement. A commonly used definition of quality taken from ISO 8402 is reproduced below.

> ***Quality*** *is the totality of features and characteristics of a product or service that bear on its ability to satisfy stated or implied needs.*

In an environment where custom software is being developed, the needs are often stated within a contract between the supplier and customer (Section 9.1 - Siemens Nixdorf Application Software and Chapter 10 - Data Logic). In a standard product environment, implied needs must be identified and defined within a requirements specification. These needs may change over time which identifies the requirement for configuration and change control of specifications. The needs are translated into features and characteristics of the software system which are expressed in terms of usability, safety, reliability, maintainability, etc.

The quality definition is not very useful to the developer of a software system. The developer is interested in learning how to develop a product that exhibits 'good' quality. For the software developer it is necessary to identify aspects of quality such that its presence or absence can be recognized. Metrics are a tool to help quantify aspects of quality such that the effect of actions to improve quality can be measured.

These quality aspects can be measured with different views of quality. A positive view of quality aspects would ask the question, how good is this product or process? Metrics can be defined by collecting opinions on the goodness of the product quality. These opinions can be quantified in terms of response classes. This positive view of quality aspects can lead to the definition of *subjective* metrics (Section 4.6.2).

A negative view of quality aspects would focus on identifying what is wrong with the product or process. Thus one could view quality by the number of deficiencies that are contained within the product or development process. Metrics that are defined using this negative view of quality aspects could include measures of the number of faults or bugs discovered in the product during different development life-cycle phases. For many developers this negative view may be easier to implement since it is easier to quantify and it has less dependence on subjective opinions. This view can lead to the definition of *objective* metrics (Section 4.6.1).

Another characteristic of quality that is important for software system developers to understand is that it is a core characteristic that has an effect on many other characteristics of the software product and development process (Figure 3.1). Improving quality will usually have a secondary improvement impact on product functionality and product implementation effort and time. For example, it has been observed by the companies whose best practices are described in this book (Chapters 9-14) that efforts to improve quality have resulted in more productive development teams and shorter product development schedules. Thus the improvement of quality should be a primary goal for development organizations wishing to improve their performance over time.

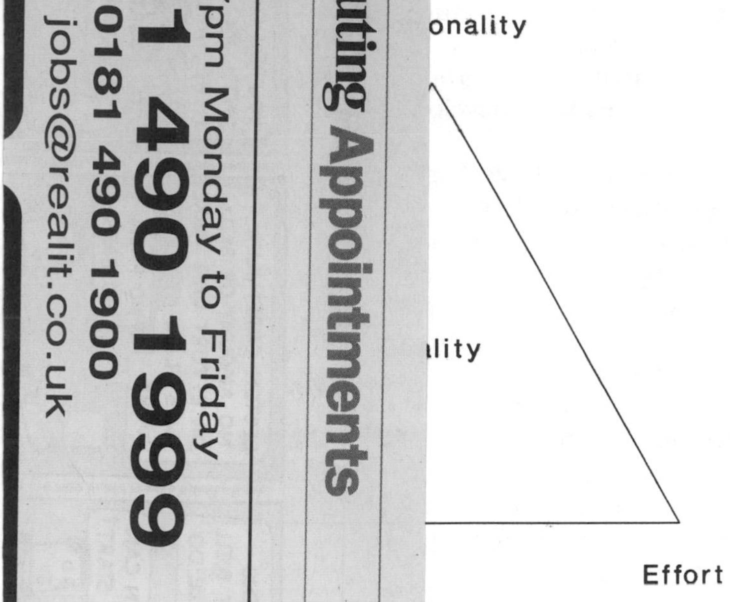

Quality Impacts.

ity

An example metric for development team productivity is defined in Chapter 6. This metric is a simple measure of the product size divided by the effort required to develop the product. The metric does not provide sufficient insight into the impact that quality has for improving productivity.

The introduction of the concepts of *efficiency* and *effectivity* may increase understanding of how better quality helps improve productivity. *Efficiency* is the ability 'to do things right'. Good efficiency implies that the software developers perform their activities correctly. They make fewer mistakes. Thus they spend less time in correcting their mistakes, and the product is developed faster.

Effectivity is the ability 'to do the right things'. Good effectivity implies that the software developers are performing the correct activities. These correct activities could include good practices of software development. Good effectivity could also mean that the developers are working on a product that when completed will be useful to the customers. Thus high quality in specifying the functional requirements of the product will improve the effectivity of the development team in developing the right product for the market.

A simplified example of how these concepts relate can be made by comparing software development work habits in the USA and Germany. As a general rule, we have observed that the software development teams in the USA tend to exhibit higher productivity than teams in Germany. This is primarily a consequence of the fact that there are more effort-hours in a staff-year in the USA due to fewer vacation days as compared to Germany. Also many software engineers in the USA as 'Exempt Employees' contribute 'Casual Overtime' to their projects, which is usually unpaid additional effort beyond the normal forty-hour work week. Casual overtime is not as common among German software engineers where it is indirectly discouraged by custom and legislation. On the other hand, software engineers in the USA tend to switch jobs and companies more frequently than in Germany. Thus the time that a team of software developers have worked together on the same applications tends to be longer in Germany than the USA. This increased development team experience results in German teams exhibiting better efficiency and effectivity as compared to teams in the USA. These examples are oversimplified generalizations based upon limited observation. However, the cultural variables within different countries that influence software development team productivity, efficiency, and effectivity is an interesting subject that warrants further investigation (Jones, 1991).

3.3 Business Objectives

The initiation of a Software Metrics Program will provide assistance to assessing, monitoring, and identifying improvement actions for achieving a set of company quality and productivity goals. The goals are established to be consistent with and supportive of the business needs of the company. The goals identify the quality and productivity improvements which are desired to be achieved within a specified time-frame or planning horizon.

Software metrics should aid in the assessment of current corporate capabilities. They can also be used to monitor the progress over time towards achieving the necessary business goals for improved quality and productivity. Software metrics are of interest for several reasons (Gafney, 1981).

- Quantitative measures can be used as indicators of a software product or development process. These indicators, such as size, product quality, process quality, etc., are of interest to software development managers, developers, and users.

- The software metrics may indicate suggestions for improving the software development process.

The quantitative data collected should be used as an indicator of development process problem areas. As a result, improvement actions can be identified and implemented. These actions can be compared and analyzed with respect to the best return-on-investment for the business unit. The measurement data provides information for investing wisely in tools for quality and productivity improvement.

The metrics play a key role in setting up a closed-loop feedback mechanism within which incremental improvements to the software development process can be made over time. These process improvements result in higher quality software system products and increased development team productivity, which in turn increases the competitiveness of the business enterprise.

3.4 Uses of Metrics

The success stories in this book describe six primary uses of metrics. They include goal-setting, improving quality, improving productivity, project planning, managing, and improving customer confidence.

3.4.1 Goal-Setting

Metric data is useful for establishing quantitative improvement objectives for company management. For example, if a business enterprise goal is to double the current development team productivity within three years, then it is desirable to define a metric which measures productivity improvement progress. The metric can be used to measure the current productivity. It can then be applied periodically to track progress until the goal is obtained. If sufficient progress is not made and the goal is not achieved, additional actions and investments can be identified and implemented for more improvement. If the goal is achieved, a new goal for the next time-period can be identified. The realism or ambitiousness of the goal will depend greatly on the company and country culture (Section 4.3).

3.4.2 Improving Quality

Metric data can be very useful when used in conjunction with a corporate quality improvement program such as one implemented using the techniques of Total Quality Management (TQM) (Feigenbaum, 1983). The quality improvement program will identify goals and desired improvements in overall quality over a specified time period. The goals of software quality improvement should be consistent with and supportive of the overall corporate quality improvement program. The software metrics should support the desired improvements for software quality. The metrics will provide an indicator of current status, and they will measure progress in achieving the goals over time.

3.4.3 Improving Productivity

Software metrics can also be applied to supporting a productivity improvement program in a manner similar to a quality improvement program. Although usually gains in quality improvement will also result in increases in productivity, direct goals and activities for improving productivity should be established. Productivity improvement is often critical to the success of the business enterprise, since it will reduce costs and increase sales with products being delivered to the market quicker. This will result in better margins and increased profitability.

3.4.4 Project Planning

The collection of metric data will improve over time the organization's skill in planning new projects. Metric data collected on prior projects will be available to project managers responsible for estimating complexity, schedule, required personnel resources, and budgets. Comparisons can be made between the proposed new project and prior similar projects. In this manner better estimates can be obtained which will improve the overall ability to plan the various business activities of the company. For example, better project schedule estimates will improve the planning associated with activities concerned with product sales introductions and replacement of older products by newer products. Better business decisions can be made concerning which proposed projects should be funded and initiated. Better return-on-investment projections can be made if better product development effort estimates are developed.

3.4.5 Managing

Software metrics are useful for managing and monitoring software projects. If metric data is made available to software project managers on a frequent basis, corrective actions can be made to the project plan to increase the probability of successful completion of the project (Andersen, 1990). For example, if the metric data includes the number of faults identified at system testing and the number appears relatively high, then it may be prudent to continue with additional testing or perhaps to rework certain components of the software before proceeding to user acceptance or pilot testing.

3.4.6 Improving Customer Confidence

A successful Metrics Program will ultimately result in higher quality software system products which will in turn increase customer satisfaction. It is also important, however, that customers have confidence in a company's ability for *potentially* delivering a high quality product. A customer's perception of a company and its services is a result of a complex series of interactions and communications, many of which are unplanned and from indirect sources. A Metrics Program can increase customer confidence by showing that the company has good knowledge of the strengths and weaknesses of its products and development process, and that it is taking positive actions to correct its weaknesses.

The Metrics Program is also useful for improving the confidence of internal customers. Internal customers are organizations within the enterprise that depend on the output of another organization.

For example, a sales organization depends on the output of engineering and manufacturing organizations to produce products for sale. The sales organization is thus an internal customer of engineering and manufacturing. Often the most demanding internal customer within a business enterprise is the management of the company. At Siemens Medical Electronics (Paulish, 1990a), it was observed that management confidence in the engineering organization increased as a result of the Metrics Program, which increased the visibility of the various product development activities. This was achieved via periodic reports which quantified product development activities such that achievements and problem areas became more obvious.

3.5 Conclusion

The uses of software metrics must be applied to supporting the objectives of the business enterprise. Metrics should only be used when specific goals for improving software quality and productivity have been identified. The general uses of metrics are summarized in Table 3.1.

Table 3.1 Uses of Software Metrics

1. Goal-Setting
2. Improving Quality
3. Improving Productivity
4. Project Planning
5. Managing
6. Improving Customer Confidence

4 Metrics Introduction Program Approach

4.1 Introduction

A number of suggestions are made concerning the approach for implementing a Metrics Program. The material is presented in the steps that a typical Metrics Program implementation would follow.

The general approach that is suggested is to begin with a documented baseline software development process which will be dynamically improved over time. Goals are established with respect to the desired improvement areas. Targets for the desired extent of quality and productivity improvements over a specified time period are identified. Metrics are then defined that can be used to measure periodic progress in achieving the improvement goals. The metric data collected is used as an indicator of development process problem areas, and actions are identified for improvement. Thus a closed-loop feedback mechanism is established which ultimately improves the software product development process resulting in higher quality products and increased development team productivity.

The approach for introducing software metrics can be described by the following seven steps:

1. Software Development Process

2. Goals

3. Responsibility

4. Initial Research

5. Metrics Definition

6. Sell

7. Feedback and Process Improvement

The approach can be applied to a company, an organization within the company, or a specific project. For companies with limited experience on software development process and metrics, it may be useful to begin small with a selected project, and then broaden the scope of the Metrics Program to additional projects as positive experience increases. The approach can be refined based on experience, and the scope of the Program gradually extended until it embraces the entire organization. Experience with this approach is given in Section 9.6.

It is assumed that the initiators of a new Metrics Program understand the basic foundations of measurement. Topics such as objectives of measurement, measurement scales, measurement data analysis, operations on measures, etc. can be found in (Fenton, 1991) within the context of software measurement. It is also useful for the Metrics Program initiators to review the experience and recommendations found in (Grady, 1987) upon which this Metrics Introduction Program approach is based. Note also that the term *metric* is not used within the strict mathematical definition. Rather, *metric* is used to define measurements for software project management.

4.2 Software Development Process

A Metrics Program will provide trend data which can be used to identify improvement opportunities for an existing software product development and maintenance process. The Metrics Program will be tightly coupled to the development process, since the metrics will be defined so as to measure performance characteristics at selected points within the process. It is therefore a prerequisite that a software development process be in place before the Metrics Program is initiated. The software development process should be documented, understood, and followed by the product development activities. The initial process need not be perfect. It is more important to have a *documented* imperfect process upon which one can *improve over time.* If no written process exists, an appropriate starting point may be to document the practices currently used for developing software products, or adapt an existing set of procedures (e.g. ISO 9000-3, IEEE) for the specific corporate environment. Software metrics should be a part of the overall strategy for software product development process improvement.

The software development process is often described by a life-cycle model. In general the process consists of a sequential series of phases separated by reviews. The reviews determine whether the current phase activities have been satisfactorily completed, and a decision is made concerning proceeding to the next phase. The life-cycle model begins at the initial product conception, and continues until the product is phased out. A software life-cycle model that has been commonly used since the early 1970s is the waterfall model (Royce, 1970). The software development activities for each phase are described for each organization. More modern software development process models are described in (Humphrey, 1991) and (Madhavji, 1991).

A promising unique approach to software development is Cleanroom Engineering (Selby, 1987; Cobb, 1990). The Cleanroom Software Engineering process utilizes separate development and testing teams, and it extensively utilizes metrics such as the Mean-Time-To-Failure (MTTF) measured during certification testing. Although measurement of projects that have used Cleanroom practices exhibit improvements in product quality and development team productivity, its application is not yet widely used in industry.

Siemens has developed a generalized software development process model that is tailored by each business dependent on the product application and culture (Chapter 9). The process model consists of four process phases which are further subdivided into eight process steps. It is general enough to apply to both hardware and/or software product development. In addition to the process steps, the functional organizations are indicated so that each organization is given general guidance on activities that should be performed within each process step. A summary of the Siemens process model is given in Figure 4.1.

After the software development process is in place for a specific organization, metrics can be used (Step 5) to provide insights on improving the process (Step 7). Thus the software development process will be incrementally improved and updated. Although the process is modelled as a series of sequential steps, improvements in reducing the time schedules to develop new products will be obtained by exploiting overlapped and parallel tasks during the development. For example, Siemens Private Communication Systems (Chapter 9) uses a technique called *phase anticipation* to help reduce the risk associated with design decisions. The various project planning and scheduling tools provide the capability for overlapping tasks and analyzing the critical path schedule.

The important characteristics of the software development process for the Seven-Step Metrics Introduction Program are that the process is documented, understood and used by the developers, and it is incrementally improved over time.

Organization

Phase	Planning		Implement.		Test		Maint.	
Step	Rqmts	HLD	Detail Design	Coding	Integ.	System Test	Field Intro.	Syst. Maint.
Product Planning	Rqmts Spec.						New Version Identification	
Project Mngt.	Proj. Plan		Project Monitoring & Control				Prod. Rel.	Vers. Plan
Engr.	Trade. Analy.	HLD Spec	Detail Des. Spec.	Code & Unit Test	Integ. Test	Fault Corr.	Supp.	Fault Corr.
Productn.			Planning			Pilot	Production	
Testing		Test Concpt	Test Plan	Test Devel.	Tst Pln Review	System Test	Field Fault Review	
Service			Service Concept		Pilot Plan	Pilot	Maintenance	
Quality Assurance	Qual. Plan		Reviews			Fault Mon.	Field Fault Review	

Figure 4.1 Product Development Process Model.

4.3 Goals

The implementation approach begins with the identification of goals for the Metrics Program. The goals of product quality and development team productivity improvement should be described in accordance with the terminology of the specific corporate environment. The goals should be derived from and consistent with the overall business goals of the organization. Quantitative goals of what improvements are expected to be achieved in a specific time period should be identified. For example, Terry Lautenbach, who is an IBM Senior Vice President and IBM US General Manager, identified goals for IBM US to achieve a tenfold reduction in defects in 1991, a hundredfold reduction in 1993, and Six Sigma performance in 1994 (Lautenbach, 1990). Six Sigma performance results in a product yield of 99.99966%, corresponding to 3.4 defective parts per million. A summary of the IBM Goals is given in Table 4.1. Summaries of the goals of HP, AT&T, and Siemens Medical Electronics (SME) are given in Tables 4.2, 4.3, and 4.4 respectively. It is important to create a vision of what the company's or organization's quality performance will be at five or more years in the future. The business goals must be considered when defining the goals for software quality and productivity improvement.

Table 4.1 IBM R&D Goals (Lautenbach, 1990)

	Market-Driven Quality Objectives				
	1990	*1991*	*1992*	*1993*	*1994*
Defect Elimination	-	10X Reduction	-	100X Reduction	Six Sigma Company
Baldrige Discipline	Rate Orgs.	New>875	All>875	Win Qualified	-
Customer & Business Partner Satisfaction	-	Gain on the Leaders	Equal to the Best	World Class	Highest in the World

Table 4.2 HP R&D Goals (John Young, April 24, 1986)

10 X GOAL

'I want us to achieve a tenfold improvement in two key software quality measures in the next five years.

The first is aimed at our design process; the second, at our ability to solve problems once customers have our products in place.

We will measure these improvements by:

1. Post-release defect density

2. Open Critical and Serious KPRs.'

Table 4.3 AT&T R&D Quality Goals

R&D Goals
10 - IN - 5

1. Reduce number of software faults found after delivery to system test by factor of ten in five years.

2. Reduce number of hardware and device design changes after ready-to-manufacture by factor of ten in five years.

3. Document quality plans for all projects.

Table 4.4 Siemens Medical Electronics Quality Goal

R&D Quality Goal

The goal of R&D Quality is to achieve a *tenfold improvement* of R&D performance within five years (37% less defects per year).

The Metrics Program objectives should be reviewed for consistency with any existing higher level corporate or organizational initiatives on quality improvement for general, not necessarily software specific activities. The expectations of the Metrics Program, in terms of anticipated improvements, should be defined and reviewed as part of the initial research. This will help to build consensus, and establish if the organization believes that the goals are realistic. Asking people what they want and what they can contribute helps to win their support of the Metrics Program. The needs and plans must be consistent with the overall aims of the organization and expressed using the local jargon.

The degree of difficulty in achieving the goals will be dependent on the company and country culture. For example, in the United States quality improvement goals are often described as *targets;* i.e., goals that are strived for but may never be actually achieved (e.g. zero defects). If major progress is made in approaching the target, the quality improvement program is considered a success. In Germany, goals are often more realistic and precise. The goals must be achieved as specified for the quality improvement program to be considered a success. It is important for the Metrics Program participants to understand the success criteria with respect to goals that are expected to be met or rather targets that will be strived for and only approached.

4.4 Responsibility

The assignment of responsibility for the introduction and implementation of the Metrics Program is an important decision point within the Seven-Step Introduction Program approach. The selection of the organizational responsibility and the individual(s) to implement the Program will be an indicator of the importance of the Program to the overall organization. Some of the desirable characteristics of the leader of the Metrics Program are summarized below.

- **Enthusiasm**. The Metrics Program leader must be enthusiastic about the potential benefits of the application of metrics to the organization. He must become a 'Project Champion' for the Metrics Program.

- **Marketing Orientation.** Since the Metrics

Program will ultimately result in substantial procedural changes and corporate or organizational cultural changes, it is important that the leader have skill in selling the concept of the Program to others. There must be an appreciation of who the 'customers' are, and what will positively motivate them to implement the tasks associated with the Program.

- **Good Communication Skills.** The Metrics Program leader should have both good written and verbal communication skills. A number of presentations will be required to help 'sell' the Program and provide the initial training. Procedures will need to be written that are easily understood and followed. The Program leader should possess the characteristics of a good teacher.

- **Good Planning Skills.** The Metrics Program leader should possess good planning skills, and have a clear vision of where the Program should be headed in the future. He should have experience in planning the tasks that will be required for a multi-year project.

- **Diplomacy.** The Metrics Program leader will be required to interface with many different organizations and individuals with conflicting goals. For example, the Marketing Group may have a goal of short development time while the Test Group is only interested in achieving zero faults. The Program leader will be required to negotiate these apparent conflicts such that the various functions work together for achieving the common goal of higher quality products.

- **Credibility.** The Program leader must possess a high degree of a priori credibility such that there will be more likelihood of cooperation with the various organizations for implementing the proposed activities. The activities should be accepted as having value to improve the organization. To maximize credibility, it is desirable that the Metrics Program leader possess substantial experience in developing software products similar to those of the organization. Ideally, the best candidates could come from existing software project managers who have demonstrated interest and experience in product development process improvement.

- **Attention to Detail and Precision.** The Metrics Program leader will be required to define a set of metrics that may substantially impact the current work habits of the existing staff. It is thus important that the proposed metrics are precisely defined and detailed enough for good initial understanding. A Program plan that is too superficial or contains basic inaccuracies will possibly be attacked by the technical organizations so as to jeopardize the successful launching of the Program.

- **Organization Skills.** The Program leader will be dealing with many people, organizations, and data. It is important that the diverse set of tasks required for Program success are well organized.

- **Persistence.** It is important that the Program leader does not get easily discouraged, and that he is committed to the Metrics Program for the long term. The Program will require years of measurements and improvements to have a significant impact on the company. Initial improvements may be substantial, but the relative gains may decrease as the obvious easier improvement actions are implemented.

- **Power.** The Program leader must be positioned within the organization such that his activities are taken seriously. Management interest and support are necessary for success of the Metrics Program. The Program leader must possess enough stature within the organization so as to reflect the support of upper management.

The Metrics Program leader will need to be both patient and innovative, and a historian of past performance data for progressively leading the Metrics Program over time. He must be capable of supporting business and project management in achieving the desired goals established for software quality and productivity improvement.

4.5 Initial Research

Once responsibility has been assigned, the initial information for establishing the Metrics Program should be collected. A recommended technique for achieving this is through a survey of internal customers. The data for the survey of internal customers can be obtained through interviews in which the internal customers are asked about their expectations concerning the Metrics Program and how they would propose measuring success. A sample questionnaire designed for a one-hour internal customer interview used at Siemens Medical Electronics Research and Development Department is given in Table 4.5. The contact and information obtained by the survey interviews will be useful later when the Metrics Program is 'sold' for initial approval and cooperation.

Another approach to gather initial data would be to perform an assessment of the current practices (Humphrey, 1987, 1989; SEI, 1991). The data obtained from the assessment could then be used to identify the initial target development process improvement opportunities and metrics selection. It is not suggested that an extensive amount of time be dedicated to the initial research step. It is better to perform a short duration assessment and get the Metrics Program started earlier. More thorough assessments and reassessments can be better performed when metrics data is available.

Table 4.5 Internal Customer Survey Questionnaire

R&D Quality

Name:
Date:

1. What is your definition of R&D Quality?

2. How good a job is the R&D Department doing?
   What is done well?
   What can be improved?

3. What measures of R&D Quality can you think of?

4. How effective is the R&D Department with working with other Corporate Departments?

5. How effective is the company in meeting overall quality goals?

Other broader assessment techniques which can lead to insights concerning the current software development process include the ISO 9000 Series guidelines and the Baldrige Award. The ISO 9000 Series (ISO 9000, 9001, 9002, 9003, 9004, 9000-3) is a set of quality management system guidelines. Specifically the ISO 9000-3 is a guide to the application of quality systems to software development. A number of companies provide as a service an audit of an organization's quality systems with the goal of independent certification. These audits can provide insights to the organization concerning discrepancies and deficiencies of the documented quality system. Successful trade in the European market for information technology requires providing evidence that the quality management system complies with the ISO 9000 requirements.

The Malcolm Baldrige Award is a national quality award for companies in the USA. Companies participating in the award process submit applications which include completion of an award examination. Applicants are expected to provide information and data on their quality processes and quality improvement. The award examination is designed to be not only the basis for making awards, but also to permit self-assessment of overall quality management.

4.6 Metrics Definition

An initial small number of metrics should be selected to be consistent with the existing software development process and the organization/project objectives. The basic set of metrics should be of a limited number in order to maximize the visibility of each measurement, and consist of *objective* and/or *subjective* measurements. Those who have had successful Metrics Programs recommend picking several easily understood and readily available metrics to start. This makes it easier to explain the Program, and avoids creating opposition such as 'more paperwork to keep us off the real job'.

4.6.1 Objective Metrics

Objective metrics are easily quantified and measured. Examples of objective metrics are:

- **Program Size.** This basic metric is primarily used as a normalizing factor for other measurements, and is used to derive meaningful quality and productivity indicators. It can thus be used to set other metrics in perspective (e.g. faults per thousand lines of code). This measurement can be made by counting lines of code or using function points (IFPUG, 1990). However, there is no ideal standard for this category. Commonly used rules for code counting are found in (Boehm, 1981) and (IEEE, 1990b). An automated tool may be useful for counting. The important point is not the unit used, but the fact that this measurement be well defined and applied consistently. This category may also imply program complexity since bigger programs are usually more complex.

- **Effort.** This measure is the primary data used for project management, but also for productivity indicators. It can be counted as staff-days or project cost depending on the existing accounting systems of the company.

- **Schedule.** This measure is the primary data used for project management, but also for process quality indicators. Elapsed time for a phase or phases can be measured, depending on the company's product development process life-cycle.

- **Number of Faults.** The number of faults is a primary indicator of product quality and can be counted at various phases of the software development life-cycle including after initial customer delivery. The definition of a fault and the time period for counting the faults must be specified. For further refinement, faults can be counted during design and coding through reviews, during testing, or during field use (customer change requests).

- **Quality Costs.** The costs associated with quality can be counted and tracked. These costs can consist of three types: Prevention, Appraisal (Test) and Failure. Failure costs can be tracked before (Internal), and after (External) customer delivery.

These *basic* metrics, after having been defined and implemented, can become the basis for a hierarchy of *additional* metrics, some of which may be *calculated*. An example of a calculated metric would be faults detected divided by the number of thousand lines of code. Basic metrics, such as customer change requests, could be expanded into additional metrics such as the number of customer complaints per thousand lines of code, complaints broken down into severity classes, and complaints per time period. Also, for example, program complexity can be measured from static code analysis using such calculations as McCabe's Metric (McCabe, 1976). Associated costs or effort expended per development activity can also be counted and tracked as they are good indicators of process quality.

One of the advantages of objective metrics is that they can often be collected more cost effectively using software tools. Tools can be purchased or developed to assist in automating the data collection and calculation of metrics (Chapter 8). The metrics definitions and collection means should be described within a written Metrics Plan.

4.6.2 Subjective Metrics

Subjective metrics attempt to track less quantifiable data such as quality attitudes. An example of a subjective metric would be the measurement of customer satisfaction (Chapter 14). Data for a subjective metric would often be collected through interviews or surveys. Subjective data could be captured as response classes; e.g., excellent, good, fair, poor. These should be defined by reference points on a scale. Reference points can consist of easy-to-understand examples of the quality attributes.

The terminology used for the various types of metrics is summarized in Figure 4.2.

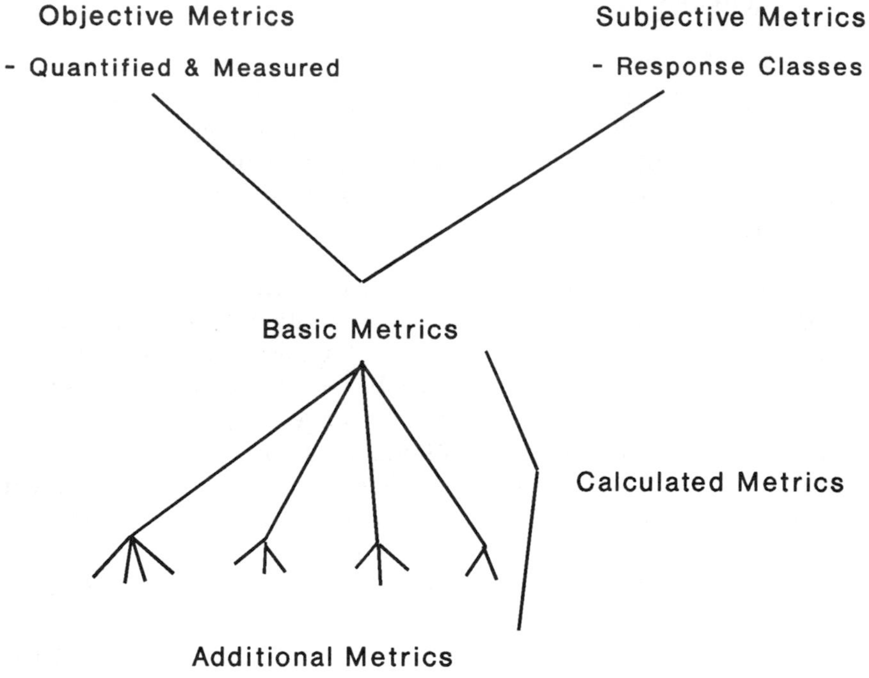

Figure 4.2 Types of Metrics.

4.6.3 Global/Phase Metrics

Metrics can be further classified into *global* or *phase* metrics. *Global* metrics are of primary interest to software managers. They are high-level indicators that may span multiple phases of the software development process. They provide insights for management concerning project status on size, product quality, and process quality. Thus they are used as a tool for software project management. It is suggested that a new Metrics Program initially establish a limited number of basic metrics which are global metrics. Additional metrics can be defined and introduced as the Program progresses.

Phase metrics are metrics that are indicators only for a specific phase of the software development process. For example, in Chapter 12, the collection of code inspection metrics is described as phase metrics for the coding phase of the software development process. Examples of global and phase metrics are given in Chapter 7. An illustration of their application to an example software development life-cycle is given in Figure 4.3.

Once a new Metrics Program is introduced and operating effectively, *additional* metrics can be introduced within a hierarchy. For example, within a phase, *additional* metrics can be defined at the lower levels of *activities* and *tasks*. Section 7.2 below provides suggestions and examples for establishing a metrics hierarchy.

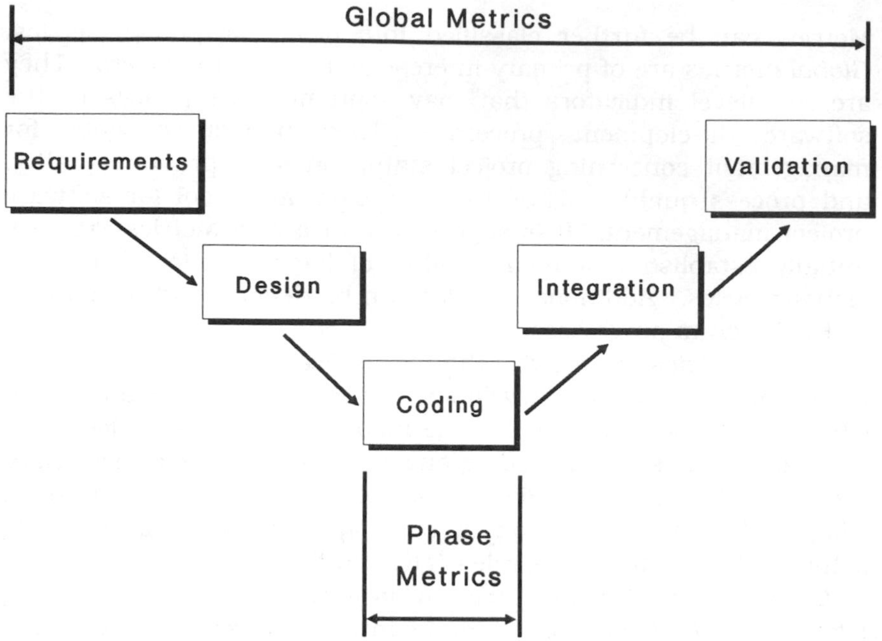

Figure 4.3 Global and Phase Metrics Applied to an Example Life-Cycle.

4.7 Sell

However different organizations may be, they are all made up of people. It is people who must make the Metrics Program work. But they must be introduced to the Program concept and persuaded. The Metrics Program concept must be 'sold' to the organization as part of the implementation approach. This is necessary in order to communicate the benefits of the Program such that a high degree of cooperation and improvement will be realized.

Different categories of organization staff will require different approaches for selling, and they will exhibit different acceptance levels. For example, upper management support is required for a successful Metrics Program. Upper management may readily accept the Program concept if a positive return-on-investment is clearly identified. Developers may accept the Program if the activities proposed result in better control and structured development procedures that reduce time and effort, and the activities do not increase work overhead. Middle management may be the most difficult 'sell' since their personal performance is often tightly coupled to their organization or project performance. Middle management should be convinced of the benefits of the proposed techniques for improving software project management. Perhaps the application of the techniques will result in fewer late nights at the office.

It may be desirable to couple the Metrics Program to an Awards Program to recognize excellent team performance. The Metrics Program must *not*, however, be applied to the measurement of individual performance. The perception of individual performance measurement could offend certain individuals and create a defensive reaction to the Program introduction. Also in some countries the use of metrics to measure individual performance may be prohibited by law.

An approach to providing the Metrics Program sales information is to establish a coordinated Training Program. The Training Program could communicate both the benefits of a metrics application as well as information on the implementation tasks.

4.8 Feedback and Process Improvement

A feedback mechanism must be implemented so that the metrics data can provide guidance for identifying actions to improve the software development process. The Program objectives identify goals to be achieved over time. The metrics measure performance with respect to the goals. For areas requiring improvement, actions are identified to strengthen the product development process. The software development process is dynamic in that the metrics provide an indicator as to which process steps can be improved. This feedback mechanism (Figure 4.4) will result in a better product development process over time.

An approach for stimulating the development process improvement actions is through the distribution of periodic reports which illustrate metrics trend data comparing current performance with past performance. The reports should contain the presentation of metrics data in convenient and meaningful formats such as histograms, trend curves, pie charts, etc.

The feedback and process improvement step is the most important step in the Seven-Step Metrics Introduction Program approach. Continuous improvements to the software development process result in higher quality products and increased development team productivity. The process improvement actions must be managed and controlled so as to achieve dynamic process improvement over time.

The types of improvement actions that could be implemented to improve the development process can be quite diverse depending on the metrics data, development environment, and available resources. Example actions can range from tools procurement to training to methods such as design review processes. Specific examples of actions taken by industrial development organizations are given in Chapters 9-14.

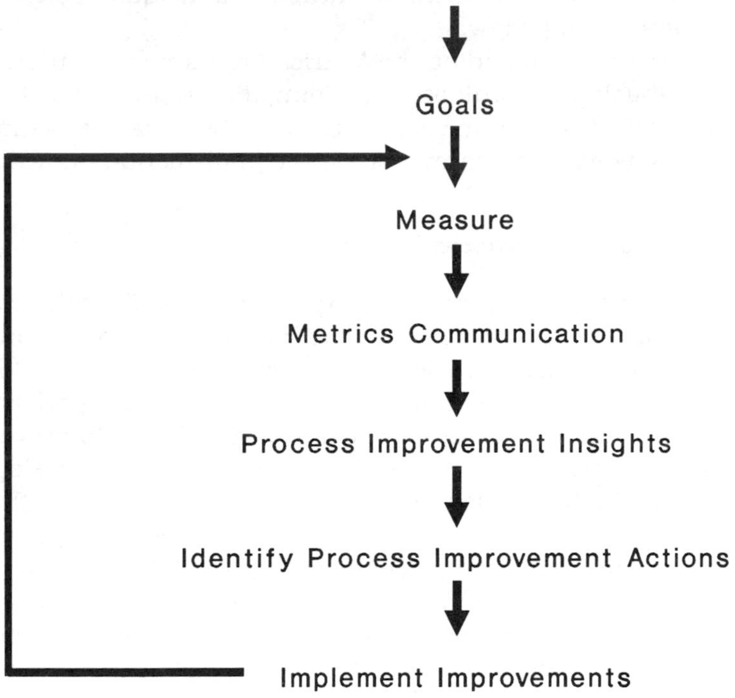

Figure 4.4 Feedback and Process Improvement.

4.9 Implementation Approach Summary

The steps involved in implementing a Metrics Program are summarized below.

1. ***Software Development Process.*** Establish and document the existing software development process. This will be the baseline process which will be measured and incrementally improved.

2. ***Goals.*** Identify the target improvement goals which are derived from and supportive of the strategic business objectives.

3. ***Responsibility.*** Identify management responsibility for the Metrics Program, and provide the organizational cultural support and visibility.

4. ***Initial Research.*** Validate the goals and customer expectations through internal customer survey and/or assessment.

5. ***Metrics Definition.*** Define the initial basic set of metrics for measuring goal achievement progress.

6. ***Sell.*** Introduce and communicate the Metrics Program to the organization such that high visibility and cooperation is achieved.

7. ***Feedback & Process Improvement.*** Identify the metrics reporting and feedback mechanisms such that software development process improvement actions can be determined and implemented.

5 Common Implementation Problems

5.1 Lack of Acceptance

The software organization may not readily accept the concept or the implementation of a Metrics Program. This is often a result of a perception that additional control and effort requirements are being placed on software development staff without their participation in the planning of the Metrics Program. Some of the specific reasons for lack of acceptance that are often given are listed below.

- ***Metrics May Restrict the Creative Process:*** Many software people consider themselves as artists involved in a creative process. Metrics may be viewed as a futile attempt to quantify an unquantifiable process. This perception needs to be overcome through example metrics and experience. Metrics are necessary to help change software development from a 'craft' to engineering within a continually improved process.

- ***Metrics Will Create Additional Work:*** Keeping records of metrics data will involve additional effort. This additional effort must be planned with the realization that time and money will be saved on the overall product development life-cycle.

- ***Benefits Are Not Clear:*** Minimal acceptance of metrics may occur when it is not well understood why they are being introduced. The benefits of quantitative approaches must be clearly explained to the organization.

- ***Fear of Being Measured:*** Many people have an inherent fear of being measured dating back to examinations and report cards from their school days. It must be pointed out that the metrics by themselves have no value; rather, it is the process improvement actions that are taken as a result of the metrics that have value to the organization.

- ***Difficulty in Admitting That Improvement is Necessary:*** Many people will assume that since quality and productivity must be improved, that there are currently existing problems. Their defense of the current process may limit the acceptance of the Metrics Program. It must be pointed out that improvement is always possible, and metrics provide insights over time as to where process improvements have the most benefit.

Overcoming a lack of acceptance is achieved by the sixth step - *Sell* - of the Seven-Step Introduction Program Approach. The benefits and goals of the Metrics Program must be clearly indicated and everyone in the organization must be trained on the application of quantitative approaches.

5.2 Personnel Appraisal

A common, often unstated, cause for lack of acceptance of metrics is the fear that metrics will be used for personnel appraisal by measuring individual performance rather than organization performance. This is particularly difficult for middle management or project management where the individual's performance is often tightly coupled to the organization or project performance.

Individual skills or attitudes are sometimes poorly matched to the requirements of the organization. Also individuals with poor productivity or poor quality work habits hurt the overall performance of the organization. It is the responsibility of management to improve the performance of such individuals or remove them from the organization.

A software project management practice at Hitachi is the 'Don't Withdraw' policy (Matsubara, 1991). This policy is supported by the belief that a person's experience will increase only if their work on a project is completed, and they see the results of their actions. Thus the policy discourages removing an individual from the project as a consequence of sloppiness or mistakes.

It is our experience that success of the Metrics Program requires independence from the Personnel Appraisal System. The purpose of metrics is to assist in improving the software development process. Its purpose is *not* to measure individual performance. It is our experience that any perception that metrics data is being used to identify poor performers within the organization will negatively impact the acceptance and success of a new Metrics Program.

A very well-established Metrics Program might be able to effectively utilize productivity and quality data to help assess individual performance. However, the data should only be used as supporting information. The immediate supervisor's assessment of the individual's performance should be used for performance appraisal, and the Personnel Appraisal System should be independent of a Metrics Program for quality and productivity improvement.

5.3 Quick Fixes - Unrealistic Expectations

A Metrics Program results in incremental improvements to the development process which are implemented over time. Thus by its nature a Metrics Program is not an appropriate approach for a quick fix to a software organization exhibiting large quality or productivity problems. A better approach for this situation is to get control of the development process and establish quality review and test bottlenecks to minimize the likelihood of bad quality products reaching the customer (Section 7.2.1).

It has been our experience that an average of two years is required to see the benefits of the Metrics Program. The benefits may also be large in the beginning with more modest gains after an initial time period since the easier obvious improvement actions are implemented first.

For success of the Metrics Program, the implementors and management must be committed to continue the program for a multi-year time period. Many of the best practices described in Chapters 9-14 have been implemented by companies for ten or more years such that metrics collection and process improvement have become part of the corporate culture and procedures. The behavior of an industrial organization changes over time. However, positive cultural changes require a combination of patience, willingness to try new ideas, and hard work.

5.4 Loss of Momentum

There is often a loss of momentum which most Metrics Programs exhibit after initial introduction. Most Metrics Programs are initially implemented with a high degree of enthusiasm and support. The enthusiasm fades, however, when much hard work is applied with minimal initial benefit. Many of the benefits are the result of cultural changes. These changes, such as instilling discipline, and staff and management education, take time to implement. Patience and good leadership are necessary to maintain the program momentum (Section 4.4).

Excellent companies have applied metrics and maintained program momentum year after year. They focused their investments and education on the weak spots indicated by the metrics, and incrementally improved their process. They achieved success by making a small improvement gain every day (Putnam, 1991).

5.5 Tools Availability

As indicated in Chapter 8, tools may have to be developed to support the collection and reporting of metrics. This requires that resources are dedicated for the selection, development, maintenance, and education of software tools that are necessary to support the software development process. Observation of Siemens companies indicates that approximately 10% of the total software staff can be dedicated to software tools development and support. This is often viewed as an extensive recurring investment by upper management, but the economic impact of a good tools group for improving the overall productivity of the software organization can be substantial.

5.6 Management Support

A successful Metrics Program must have visible management support. Management must continually reinforce the message that quality and productivity are important to the success of the organization. The support must be visibly demonstrated by actions such as award programs and stopping shipments of products that are measured as having unacceptable quality.

5.7 Poor Goals or Follow-Up

A Metrics Program can also fail if the goals of the program are not well defined, or progress towards implementing the goals is not monitored. Another common problem is failure to effectively and timely implement the process improvement actions that were indicated by the metrics.

The goals must be realistic and monitored frequently. If the goals are quickly met, new more difficult goals can be defined with a new implementation time-frame.

It must be pointed out again that metrics by themselves do nothing to improve product quality and development team productivity. The benefits come as a result of the actions which are implemented to improve the product development process. The actions must be planned, organized, and monitored with respect to their implementation completion. Resources must be planned and allocated for both personnel to accomplish the actions, and funding for the purchase of software tools, equipment, and training.

5.8 Lack of Team Players

A successful quality or productivity improvement program will require a team effort from all participants in the development process. Many specialists are required to develop software products. These specialists include developers, managers, testers, quality, and other disciplines. A high degree of cooperation is required for measuring and improving the development process.

Team players are necessary to bridge the gaps between organizations (e.g., development versus test). Contributions from individuals with diverse skills must be made within the teams assigned the responsibility to define and implement the process improvement actions. Shared values and attitudes will be necessary to build a positive quality culture within the organization.

Although certain individuals may perform better in a team environment than others, management can take many actions to encourage team participation. For example, visible cooperation between the leaders of different departments in jointly solving quality problems will give a positive role-model message to the organization. Also a management attitude of 'let's solve problems and improve' rather than 'who's to blame for this problem', will open communications between organizations and encourage team cooperation.

6 Metrics Characteristics

6.1 Software Quality Metrics Framework

6.1.1 Introduction

The Computing Services Association (CSA) Software Quality Metrics Framework (Model) is introduced as a practical approach for describing software metrics. This model was initially described in a CSA Briefing Note (CSA, 1990). The model was developed by a working party attached to the CSA Quality Assurance Group, and it has been submitted to the ISO. Contributions were made to the model by the PYRAMID Consortium member - Data Logic.

The CSA Quality Metrics Framework is one of many existing models (McCall, 1980; Basili, 1984). The CSA Model has been selected for inclusion here since it is easily understood.

There is a requirement for quality goals, as derived from the needs of the business, to be established across the phases of a selected software development life-cycle. The Software Quality Metrics Framework introduces categories of metrics that extend through the phases of a software development life-cycle which are independent of the methodology employed. The framework is designed to address a wide range of quality characteristics for software products and processes. The model enables better description of software quality aspects of products and processes so that they can be measured.

The model defines a *software quality metric* as a quantitative measure of an attribute that describes the quality of a software product or process.

6.1.2 The Model

The Software Quality Metrics Framework is defined to assist in selecting and categorizing metrics. The goals for software quality improvement, and the metrics selected to measure performance against the goals, are derived from higher level objectives; i.e., business, systems, operations, management, etc.

Three categories of metrics are defined which are independent of the software development process life-cycle phases, standards, and methodology used.

6.1.2.1 Size

This metric category establishes the size of the software product. Size can be measured in function point counts, lines of code, or effort. It is a useful metric category for helping to establish system development effort, schedules, and cost. It is also often used as a 'normalizing' factor for the quality categories described below (e.g. faults found per number of thousand lines of code).

6.1.2.2 Product Quality

This metric category characterizes the quality level of the software product or service itself. These metrics are defined during the operational life of the software. Some metrics can be 'interim' for providing insights into the final product quality or complexity, such as program or functional specification complexity. Examples of metrics in this category could include the number of faults detected and counted during System Test and the number of Customer Change Requests.

6.1.2.3 Process Quality

This category of metrics characterizes the maturity of the process within which the software product is developed. These metrics can be measured during the product development for providing real-time feedback to software project management. An example of this type of metric would be the management of development team productivity.

A pictorial representation of the Software Quality Metrics Framework as reproduced from CSA (1990) is given in Figure 6.1.

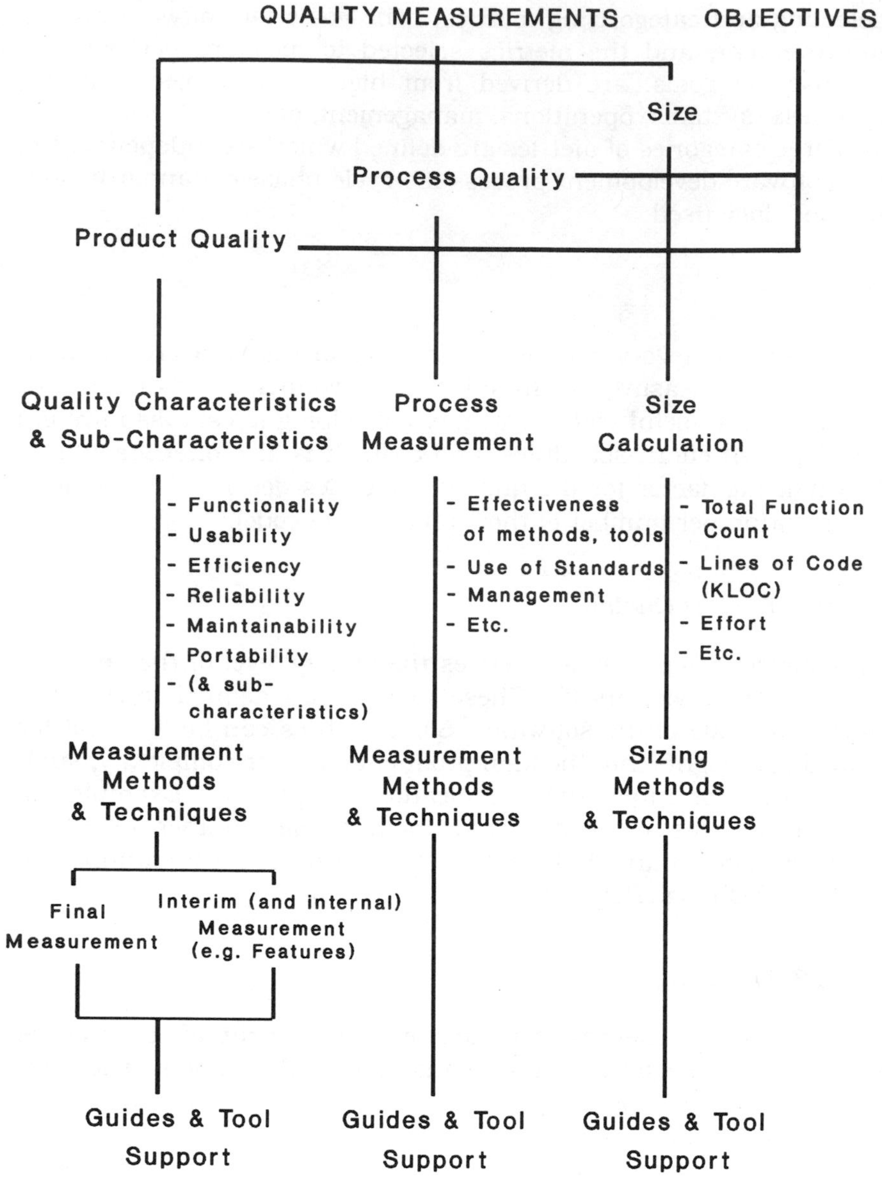

Figure 6.1 Software Quality Metrics Framework.

6.1.3 Benefits

The use of the Software Quality Metrics Framework provides the following benefits.

- The metrics are driven by business objectives, and relevant quality goals can be established at the beginning of a project. The metrics can then be tracked during the development life-cycle.

- The framework enables the assessment of the quality of the development process, and supports techniques such as the determination of the Software Engineering Institute's (SEI) questionnaire for determining development maturity level (Humphrey, 1987, 1989; SEI, 1991). This enables management and development staff to assess the progress of selected process parameters in meeting the stated business objectives. This assessment can also be used to provide an indicator of the return-on-investment associated with introducing new tools, methods, techniques, etc.

- The framework identifies the need for sizing metrics. This is useful for estimating anticipated schedule and cost requirements. The sizing data is also used to normalize the product and process quality metrics to assist in comparisons across projects within an organization.

- The model is life-cycle independent so its use is not affected by various development methodologies which may be utilized. In addition, the model can be consistently applied as the metrics data is used to incrementally improve the existing development process over time.

- The model enables the integrated use of other software quality improvement techniques such as 'Fagan style' inspections (Fagan, 1976) and the above-mentioned SEI assessment technique.

- The model consists of a simple structure (i.e.,

three categories) which is easy to remember and apply.

6.2 General Characteristics of Metrics

After the goals of the Metrics Program have been identified, responsibility has been assigned, and the initial research has been initiated, the initial basic set of metrics can be defined. The metrics will be used to measure performance with respect to the goals. This section provides guidance on the characteristics of good metrics for the purpose of the selection of metrics that are most applicable to a specific corporate development environment. It is recommended that a small number of metrics be implemented initially, and eventually a hierarchy of metrics be established such that everyone in the organization has improvement goals that can be measured using the appropriate metrics.

The characteristics of metrics can be classified into *organizational* characteristics and *technical* characteristics.

6.2.1 Organizational Characteristics

Organizational characteristics of metrics apply to the application of the metrics within a corporate organizational environment.

6.2.1.1 Application to Software Process and Project Management

The global metrics should be applied to the entire software development life-cycle. The metrics should not be restricted merely to the coding phase. The metrics will be used as a tool for achieving excellence in software project management. The metrics data will be an input for providing guidance for identifying actions to improve the software development process. It is assumed that a documented software development process exists prior to the introduction of the Metrics Program.

6.2.1.2 Highly Visible

The limited number of metrics should be visible both within and external to the organization. When there are a small number of metrics, recall of the key metrics should be simplified. It is suggested that the metrics, whenever confidentiality considerations permit, be publicly displayed in a physical area of heavy staff traffic such as a hallway or meeting area. It is also suggested that promotion and review be actively pursued through business reviews, periodic reports, newsletters, or any other public communication vehicles used within the specific corporate culture. Again it must be emphasized that the metrics are not used in performance evaluations of individuals. Public display of the metrics may lead to healthy (or unhealthy) competition between development teams depending on the tone of the display and the corporate environment.

Metric data that is collected which exhibits values much better than the norm for the organization should be publicized as 'success stories'. This will help promote the further utilization of the metrics and provide future target achievement goals.

6.2.1.3 Consistently Applied

The metrics should be applied in a consistent manner across projects over an extended period of time. The metrics should be designed to provide relative quality indication trends on an ongoing basis. Consistent measurements are necessary to establish credibility and allow comparisons among projects at different time periods within their life-cycle, such that lessons could be derived with respect to which development processes have been most successful.

6.2.1.4 Management Interest and Support

The Metrics Program must be supported and encouraged by corporate management if it is to be successful. It has been observed that many corporate staff members are 'boss watchers'. That is, if management visibly pays attention to a specific issue, staff members will often allocate their time to give higher priority to that issue. In other words, most people pay more attention to what their bosses do than to what they say. Visible participation by management in the Metrics Program is critical to its success.

6.2.1.5 Organizational Acceptance

Success of the Metrics Program is dependent upon the acceptance by the organization of the metrics that have been selected. For this reason there should be extensive review of the metrics before they are introduced as a procedure that gets incorporated into the corporate culture. The use of internal customer surveys may be a vehicle to get early acceptance of a metric that would be viewed as worthy of measurement within the organization.

6.2.1.6 Politics

It is important that the Metrics Program is not undermined by a corporate political environment that does not support the specific metrics chosen. For this reason it is important to select metrics that do not offend personal feelings or negatively impact morale (Kitchenham, 1986). The purpose of a Metrics Program is to improve over time the product development process such that higher quality products result, and the productivity of the development staff increases. The purpose of the Metrics Program is *not* to identify key individuals who could be proven to be detrimental to the well-being of the organization. As stated above, the use of metrics to measure staff personnel performance is not recommended. The metrics chosen should measure the product development process and *project team* performance. The metrics should be used as an indicator of where product development process could be improved over time.

6.2.1.7 Responsibility and Control

Metrics should be chosen such that there is clear identification of responsibility and control with respect to the individuals that have the ability and resources to improve the metric performance. There is little value to reporting a problem for which there is no one who could do anything to improve the performance associated with the problem. If the hierarchy of metrics is consistent with the organizational structure, it should be obvious which individuals have the responsibility and control to improve performance for a specific metric.

6.2.1.8 Historical Data Availability

It is highly desirable that metrics that are introduced to the organization could utilize data that has been previously collected for that organization. In this manner it will be easier to identify the current state of practice within the organization, and to identify the target goals for future performance. The availability of historical data will give the Metrics Program a 'head-start' with respect to providing initial data and establishing credibility for the metrics. One must be certain, however, that the historical data was collected using consistent counting rules over time.

6.2.1.9 Product Development Process Correspondence

The metrics chosen must correspond to the current software product development process. For example, there would be little value in attempting to collect fault data statistics for design reviews if design reviews were not commonly performed as part of the development process. Process improvements should result in better metrics values. The metrics should be used to identify areas of the development process which could be improved. Software development process improvement expertise should be coupled with metrics expertise within individuals and organizations. Within Hewlett-Packard this position is referred to as a 'Productivity Manager' (Grady, 1987). In the Japanese Software Factory, the metrics/process coupling is described by the characteristics of *Process/Quality Analysis and Control* and *Tailored and Centralized Process R&D* (Cusumano, 1991), as implemented within Hitachi's Systems Development Laboratory.

6.2.1.10 Process Opportunity Targets

The initial metrics should be chosen so as to support the initial target opportunities associated with process improvement. Not all areas of the product development process life-cycle can be improved simultaneously. A coherent plan must be developed to target areas which will initially result in the best return-on-investment. For example at Siemens Medical Electronics (Paulish, 1990b), an initial target process improvement area was validation testing, so that better quality products could be introduced to the clinical-testing activities. For this reason, there was a heavy emphasis placed on metrics which counted and calculated the number of faults detected during formal validation testing of software systems.

6.2.1.11 Patience

Metrics data must be collected over several years. Some metrics will be highly valuable and lead to many process improvement insights, and some metrics will lead to fewer insights. Initial gains may be quite extensive, but future improvements will become more difficult as the easier more obvious improvement tasks are implemented first. Patience and persistence must be characteristics of the developers of the Metrics Program.

6.2.2 Technical Characteristics

Technical characteristics of metrics apply to the definition of the metric itself.

6.2.2.1 Limited Number

It is recommended that the number of metrics that any individual in the organization needs to be concerned with is limited to five or less. This is to promote maximum concentration to a small number of improvement areas so that they are easily recalled and highly visible to the development staff. A product development organization can measure its performance with a limited number of high-level metrics for which the manager of that organization will have responsibility. For example, a product development organization may wish to define metrics which measure faults found during system testing, faults found by customers, product size, schedule adherence, and staff productivity across the projects that are within the responsibility of the manager of product development.

When the high level or basic metrics are defined and are being monitored, a number of additional metrics can be defined in a hierarchical fashion consistent with the organizational makeup of the product development activity. For example,

- the *systems engineering* function could define metrics associated with requirements definition;

- the *design* function could be concerned with metrics associated with design faults;

- the *test* function could be concerned with metrics associated with test coverage and fault detection; and

- the *documentation* function could track metrics associated with pages of documentation produced per staff-person per time period.

6.2.2.2 Easily Calculated

The metrics which are selected should be easily calculated. Real-time tracking is highly desirable such that the metrics can be used for quickly identifying or predicting when a software development process exhibits a negative trend. Thus the metrics should be simple, and require straightforward calculations for reporting and tracking. Simple calculation will also encourage individuals to monitor progress on their own rather than waiting for a periodic summary report from a centralized metrics reporting function.

6.2.2.3 Readily Available Data

The data that is used as a source for metrics calculation should be readily available. The ideal situation is to base the metrics calculations on data that is routinely reported as part of the existing corporate culture (Navlakha, 1986). Examples of desirable existing systems which could be used as a source for data collection include:

i. An automated cost accounting system used for collecting effort data on the various product development tasks.

ii. A software configuration management system that contains and controls source code and documentation. Size estimates can be quickly and easily measured from the configuration management system using simple software tools.

iii. An automated software problem reporting and tracking system for determining fault rate data, and for the analysis of the cause and possible future prevention of faults.

6.2.2.4 Precisely Defined

It is important that the metrics selected be given very precise and well-understood definitions for calculation. Ill-defined metrics will only create confusion within the product development organization, and serve as a source of frustration for both the developers and initiators of the Metrics Program.

6.2.2.5 Tools Support

It is important for the metrics chosen to be supported by readily available (purchased or developed in-house) software tools (Chapter 8). This will result in less manual effort required to collect data, calculate metrics, and display the metrics for publication. Metrics automation can significantly improve the overall cost-effectiveness of the Metrics Program. The tools must also be selected so as to support the activities of the development process.

6.2.2.6 Experimentation

It is suggested that the metrics developers cautiously experiment with metrics selection over time. Some metrics may not yield any significant information about the development process. New ideas on metrics will arise subsequent to initiation of the Program. Also, the metrics may have to be changed to be consistent with changes in the software development process. Old metrics that are no longer useful should be abandoned, and new metrics should be created to take their place.

6.2.2.7 Standards

At the current time there are few or any approved standards identified for software quality metrics. Although standards activities are in process (IEEE, 1990a; IEEE, 1990b), the identification of standards is extremely difficult due to the wide variation found in developing different types of software applications and the lack of standards associated with software development process. The current proposed standards can serve as a guideline for the developer of a Metrics Program. The specific definitions of the metrics selected should be developed in accordance with the development process and organization culture in which they will be implemented.

7 Example Metrics

7.1 Global Metrics

It is necessary to provide examples of metrics since there is currently a general lack of widely used standards for software metrics. The examples are derived from corporate standards utilized by Siemens (Möller, 1991) and Data Logic (Data Logic, 1989). The examples can be used as a starting point for initial metrics definitions for a new Metrics Program. It is anticipated that these example metrics would be modified to be consistent with the specific corporate software project development process environment.

It is important that a new Metrics Program be set up with only a *limited number* of initial basic metrics. These metrics should be precisely defined and communicated to all participants in the Metrics Program. In this manner high visibility for the basic metrics will be achieved within the organization.

The basic set of example metrics consists of five easy to collect and to interpret global metrics suitable for measuring progress in achieving quality and productivity improvement goals. By using these example metrics as a starting point, the tailoring effort necessary to fit a particular organization could be minimized.

7.1.1 Size

As described in the Software Quality Metrics Framework (CSA, 1990), size is a primary metrics category (Section 6.1). A commonly used approach for measuring program size is by counting lines of code. Unfortunately, there are no standards for this measurement, and the implied functionality of a line of code differs dependent on the implementation language. A commonly used definition for a line of code (LOC) from (Conte, 1986) is reproduced below.

> *A **line of code** is any line of program text that is not a comment or blank line, regardless of the number of statements or fragments of statements on the line. This specifically includes all lines containing program headers, declarations, and executable and non-executable statements.*

This definition is consistent with the Siemens standards as calculated by the PROLOC code counting tool (Möller, 1991), and also for the COCOMO Cost Estimation Model (Boehm, 1981). A commonly used metric for products that are in a maintenance phase is the delta lines of code. This is counted as the number of lines of code that were added or modified for a current release as compared with the prior release of a software product. Some organizations also count program statements rather than lines of code or they may count deleted lines.

The units and definitions used for counting lines of code, however, are of minor importance as long as they are consistently measured within an organization. In general, the simplest unit to measure should be chosen, and academic discussions about the respective merits of various units should be avoided.

An alternate approach to lines of code for measuring program size is Function Points (Albrecht, 1979; IFPUG, 1990). Function points are calculated by examining functional characteristics of the software system in terms of inputs, outputs, interfaces, files, and complexity. Function points have value for comparing projects written in different programming languages. Function points can also be calculated from a Requirements or Design Specification prior to the start of coding. The drawback with using Function Points is that training is required to calculate them (Dreger, 1989), and there are currently limited available automated tools for calculating them.

Based on the above we will define our first example basic metric as lines of code for measuring size.

> 1. ***Lines of Code (LOC):*** This metric is defined as the count of program lines of code excluding comment or blank lines. This metric is typically given in units of thousands of lines of code (KLOC).

7.1.2 Product Quality

A predominant measure of software quality is the counting of known faults at various points in the software development life-cycle. A goal of high quality software product development is to identify and remove as many faults as possible prior to customer delivery. Faults should be found, counted, and corrected as early as possible in the development life-cycle through the use of both test and inspection techniques. Data Logic's experience indicates that 70-80% of the total faults can be removed by inspection techniques prior to System Test. A simple definition of a fault taken from (Conte, 1986) is given below.

> *A* ***fault*** *is an error in software that causes the product to produce an incorrect result for valid input.*

Other terms that are often used with the same meaning as fault include defect, failure, bug, and error (IEEE, 1989). More precisely an error made in designing or developing the product can result in a fault or bug or defect within the specification or code. A failure occurs when a software system fails to operate correctly as defined by the software requirements specification. Thus an error can cause multiple faults, and a fault can cause multiple failures. When testing a software system operational problems are observed which may be failures. These failures must be analyzed to determine the fault within the software system that caused the failure. For the Metrics Program it is important to precisely define what will be counted as a fault and how the data will be collected. For example, should duplicate fault reports or requests for new or different functionality be counted? A set of fault-counting rules is necessary.

For our example metrics, we will count faults at two specific times within the software development life-cycle:

- System Test
- Field Use.

7.1.2.1 Product Quality Measurement During System Test

The first time that we will count faults for our example metrics will functionally testing a developed and integrated software product using a set of tests for a finite time period. The testing may be performed by an in-house organization that is independent of the development organization (e.g. Quality Assurance). It is assumed that System Test will occur prior to use of the software by any customer at a field location. We will normalize the number of faults detected for a release by dividing by the size of that release in thousand lines of code, thus making it a *calculated* metric. In addition to merely counting the number of faults, one may also define metrics which consider the fault arrival rate as a function of testing time.

Based on the above we will define our second metric as given below.

> 2. ***System Test Faults:*** This metric is calculated by dividing the total number of software faults reported by the testing function during System Test by the number of thousand lines of code for each product for each release. This is an indicator of the software quality and testing effectiveness of the software engineering function responsible for the product.

7.1.2.2 Product Quality Measurement During Field Use

The second example time point of fault measurement will be subsequent to shipment of the software product to users. For this example, we will count faults for a period of one year after the first customer installation of the product. The same fault reported by multiple users will be counted as a single fault. It is assumed that reasonable use of the product will occur during the first year of installation. That is, we will not consider the situation in which no or few faults are reported on a product because it was not used by customers.

Based on the above we will define our third example metric as given below.

> 3. ***Customer Change Requests:*** This metric is calculated by dividing the number of unique change requests made by customers for the first year of field use of a given release by the number of thousand lines of code for that release. Only

> change requests which are faults detected by the customers will be counted. Feature enhancement change requests which are beyond the functionality documented in the software requirements specification will not be counted for this example metric. This metric is a measure of pre-release testing and overall software product quality. It also may be a partial indicator of customer satisfaction.

It is highly desirable for the Customer Change Requests metric to be less than the System Test Faults metric for a given release. It is essential to minimize the number of faults that are discovered by the users of a software product. This example metric provides an indication of the amount of maintenance effort that may be required for a specific software system implementation.

The application of these product quality metrics during the software development testing life-cycle is illustrated in Figure 7.1.

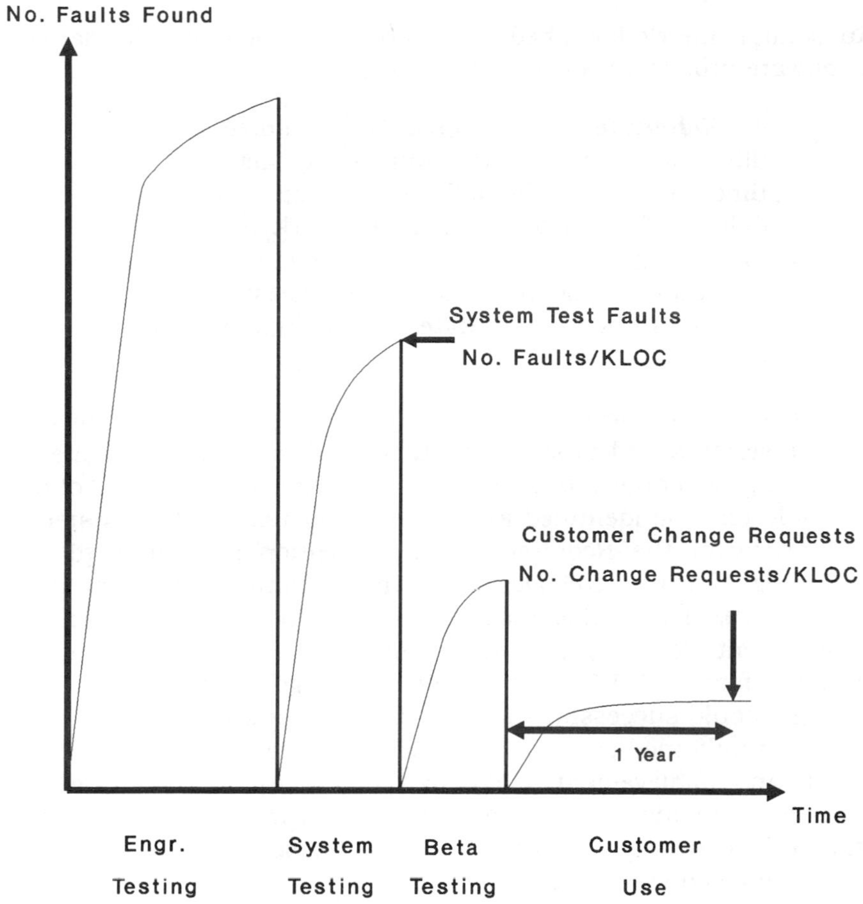

Figure 7.1 Example Product Quality Metrics.

7.1.3 Process Quality

Metrics which are of interest to management in the Process Quality category are often concerned with the efficient application of personnel resources to software product development. Two example areas of interest are:

- schedule adherence,
- development team productivity.

7.1.3.1 Schedule Adherence Measurement

An example metric for schedule adherence or the ability to manage a software project on schedule is given below.

> 4. ***Schedule:*** This metric is calculated as the difference between the planned and actual work time to achieve the milestone of first customer delivery divided by the planned work time. The metric is given as a percentage; a negative number indicates a schedule slip and a positive number indicates the actual date was achieved earlier than plan.

The Schedule metric is a measure of the organization's ability to provide services and products on time, and to meet commitments concerning schedules. It is recommended that the beginning of the schedule plan be identified as a date subsequent to the existence and review of the Requirements Specification and prior to the beginning of High-Level Design. Barry Boehm's empirical data (Boehm, 1981) indicates that at that time-point in the software development life-cycle, the software estimate should be accurate to within a factor of 1.25. It is felt that a good Software Project Manager could successfully manage this uncertainty level, perhaps through unplanned overtime. The schedule start date, uncertainty levels, and achievement goals are subject to definition by the specific company dependent on its corporate and country standards concerning labor hours and its software development process milestone reviews.

An example Schedule Metric is given in Figure 7.2. This metric only measures the ability of the development process to implement projects in compliance with the estimated schedule plan. Once this metric is under control, many organizations will want to reduce development time and define additional metrics to help streamline the development process.

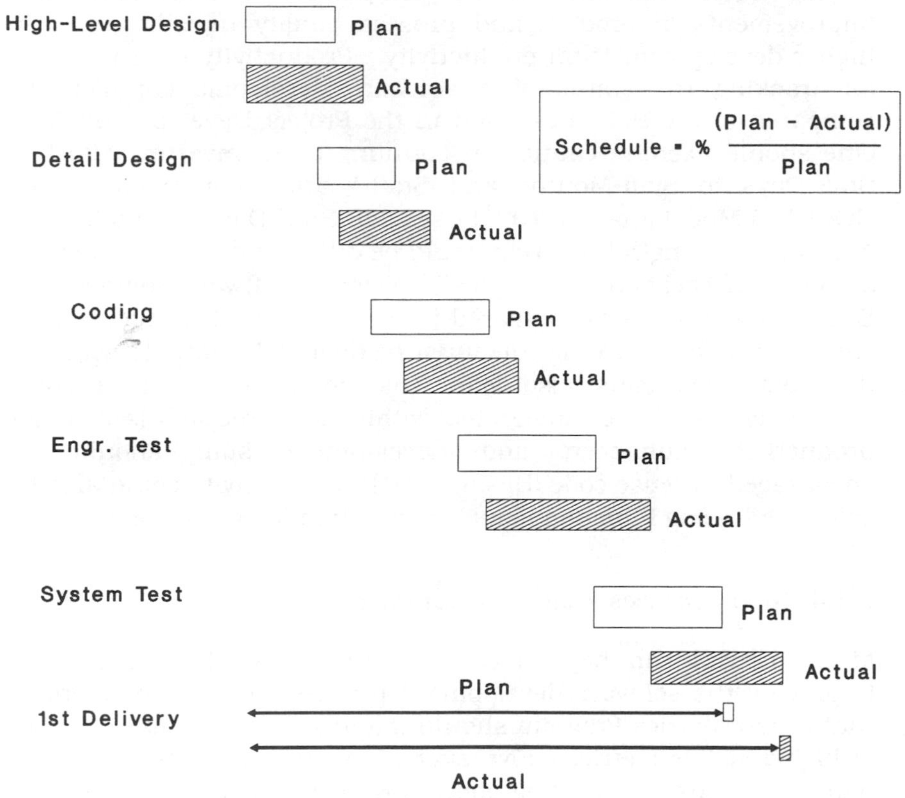

Figure 7.2 Example Schedule Metric.

7.1.3.2 Development Team Productivity Measurement

An example metric definition for software development team productivity is given below.

> 5. ***Productivity:*** This metric is calculated by dividing the number of product lines of code that were developed by the effort in Staff-Days required to develop the product. Effort is counted from the beginning of High-Level Design to First Customer Shipment. Effort includes software engineering labor as well as the effort expended for testing, reviews, project management, and documentation.

It has been observed by the companies in this book that improvements in product and process quality usually result in higher development team productivity. Productivity data is useful for tracking the status of a software development project as compared to the estimates given in the Project Development Plan. One should exercise caution in counting and converting effort in Staff-Days to Staff-Months and Staff-Years. For example, the COCOMO Model (Boehm, 1981) uses 228 Staff-Days per Staff-Year. A 'European' length Staff-Year could be different due to the varying amounts of vacation time typically given to software engineers in European countries as compared to the United States. Similarly, a consistent effort counting rule must be defined for unpaid overtime if it exists. One must also define rules for handling reused code. Previously tested code integrated within new products is a major productivity enhancer, and development staff should be encouraged to reuse code (Basili, 1991). Productivity could also be calculated using Function Points rather than lines of code.

7.1.4 Global Metrics Examples Summary

Many metrics can be defined and tracked for the purpose of improving the software development process. It is recommended that a new Metrics Program should initially define a small number of highly visible metrics. Five example metrics have been defined herein as a possible starting point for a new Metrics Program. The five example metrics are summarized in Table 7.1.

Table 7.1 Global Metrics

Metric	*Example Metrics Category*	*Units of Measurement*
1. Lines of Code	Size	KLOC
2. System Test Faults	Product Quality	No. Faults/KLOC
3. Customer Change Requests	Product Quality	No. Change Requests/KLOC
4. Schedule	Process Quality	% (Planned Work Time - Actual Work Time)/Planned Work Time
5. Productivity	Process Quality	LOC/Staff-Day

7.2 Phase Metrics

7.2.1 Metrics Hierarchy

A new Metrics Program should begin with a small number of global metrics as represented by the examples given above. The global metrics are primarily of interest to software management. Once the global metrics are defined, communicated, accepted, and monitored, a hierarchy of metrics can be defined dependent on the characteristics and goals of the software organization.

The metrics hierarchy should be designed to limit the number of metrics for which any individual has responsibility to five or less. It should be developed taking into account the organization structure and the software development process. An example matrix for designing such a hierarchy, which takes into account both phase and functional organization, is given in Table 7.2.

Table 7.2 Example Phase Metrics Matrix

	Process Phase							
Funct. Org.	*Rqmt*	*HLD*	*Det Des*	*Coding*	*EngTst*	*SysTst*	*FldT*	*Maint*
Proj. Mngt.		<--	global metric		-->			
Syst. Engr.	x	x						
Des. Engr.		x	x					
Dev. Engr.			x	x	x			
Syst. Test.						x	x	
Sust. Engr.								x

An example metrics hierarchy from Siemens Medical Electronics is given in Figure 7.3.

The priority for improvement emphasis should be given to functions and phases that will best meet the business goals. For example, if a company has a goal to build products that are more user friendly, perhaps the improvement emphasis should be put on the requirements phase under the responsibility of systems engineering.

For organizations that have overall product quality problems and limited experience with metrics, it is recommended that the improvement emphasis be put on system testing (Paulish, 1990b). In this manner the organization can at least stop poor quality products from reaching the customer. After this controlled bottleneck is established, the emphasis could be moved earlier in the process in order to prevent faults rather than test for faults after the product has been implemented. A manufacturing analogy is to put more inspection into the manufacturing process prior to packing and shipping until there is enough time available to correct upstream process problems such as poor quality incoming components.

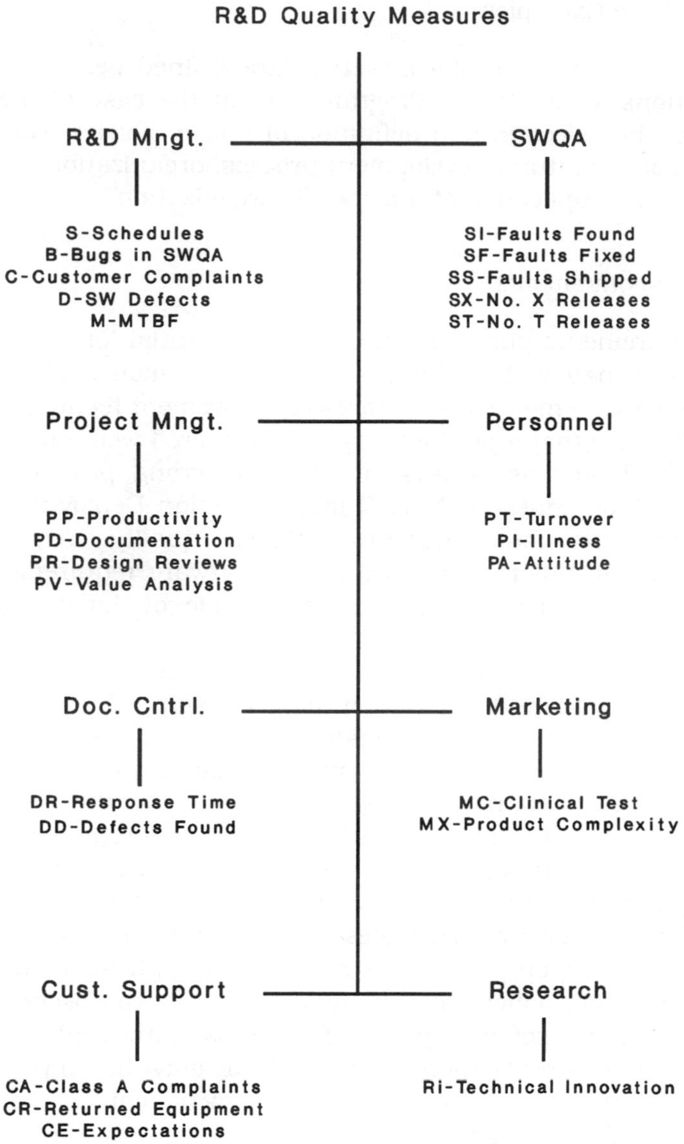
R&D Quality Measures
R&D Mngt.
S-Schedules
B-Bugs in SWQA
C-Customer Complaints
D-SW Defects
M-MTBF
SWQA
SI-Faults Found
SF-Faults Fixed
SS-Faults Shipped
SX-No. X Releases
ST-No. T Releases
Project Mngt.
PP-Productivity
PD-Documentation
PR-Design Reviews
PV-Value Analysis
Personnel
PT-Turnover
PI-Illness
PA-Attitude
Doc. Cntrl.
DR-Response Time
DD-Defects Found
Marketing
MC-Clinical Test
MX-Product Complexity
Cust. Support
CA-Class A Complaints
CR-Returned Equipment
CE-Expectations
Research
Ri-Technical Innovation

Figure 7.3 Example Metrics Hierarchy.

7.2.2 Phase Examples

A number of example phase metrics are defined below to provide suggestions for a Metrics Program. As in the case of the global metrics, the selection and definition of phase metrics will depend on the goals, culture, development process, organization structure, and product application of the specific organization.

7.2.2.1 Requirements

The requirements phase has the biggest potential for cost savings, but unfortunately this phase has the least amount of industrial experience with metrics and process improvement techniques. It is often the case that a product may be engineered well but it is not a commercial success because it was the wrong product for the market. Techniques such as Quality Function Deployment (QFD) hold promise for generating higher quality requirements specifications, but their application to software requirements has been somewhat limited in industry outside of Japan (Burrows, 1991).

It has been observed that the requirements phase often takes much longer than desired or it may be skipped entirely. The development team is usually small at this time of the life-cycle, and investment is minimal. The phase time duration should be carefully monitored, however, because it can delay the introduction of a product to the market such that a good product misses its market opportunity window. It has been shown that a fast product development time has significant competitive and financial benefits even if the development cost goes over budget (Dumaine, 1989).

The primary output of the requirements phase is usually a requirements specification document. It has been observed that a major cause for software project failures is a frequently changing requirements specification. Although it may be impossible to 'freeze' a requirements specification, it can be 'chilled'; i.e., it can be put under configuration control and proposed requirement changes can be carefully evaluated before implementing. This can help guard against the phenomena sometimes referred to as 'creeping functionality'. The cost of functional changes will increase as the project gets further downstream in the development process in terms of the amount of rework required. A major advantage of using function points is that they can be used for measuring requirements growth, and thus they can help control the revisions made to the requirements specification. A common similar problem is products that are 'overspecified' in terms of functionality such that features must be removed due to implementation complexity or little marketing value.

Based on the above, we will define our first example phase metric as the number of change requests to the functional requirements specification.

1. ***Requirements Specification Change Requests:*** This metric is defined as the number of change requests that are made to the requirements specification. Requested changes are counted from the time of the first release of the requirements specification document to the time of the beginning of product field use.

7.2.2.2 High-Level and Detail Design

Design errors or faults can be counted during the high-level and detailed design phases for a product. The faults count can be subdivided into the number for the different subsystems and modules of the product, and they can be assigned severity classes (e.g. Serious, Cosmetic, Documentation Only, etc.).

The fault data will normally be collected during design reviews. Thus the process of design reviews and fault data collection should be tightly coupled with the software development process and improved (Fagan, 1976). Examples of design quality metrics can be found in Card (1990). Our second example phase metric is defined below.

2. ***Design Faults:*** This metric is defined as the count of faults found during all design reviews in the high-level and detailed design phases for the software product.

7.2.2.3 Coding

Code faults for a software product can also be defined in a manner similar to design faults. The code faults would be counted during code reviews. This is also the phase for applying the various existing code metrics (McCabe, 1976; Halstead, 1977), which can be calculated using static code analysis tools. It is recommended that the code metrics be integrated into the organization's coding standards such that acceptable limits be defined and the metrics values reviewed within the code review process. Our third example phase metric is given below.

> 3. ***Code Faults:*** This metric is defined as the number of faults found during all code reviews for the software product.

7.2.2.4 Engineering, System, and Field Test

Keeping track of bugs and testing progress will provide insights into the testing process (Beizer, 1984). We have previously defined a System Test Fault metric as a global metric which counts the number of faults found during system testing divided by the software size.

A good way to monitor testing progress and product quality is to keep track of the rate of faults discovered per time. For example, one can plot the number of faults found per week of testing. If the rate is constant or increasing, the product should not be released to the next phase of testing or customer delivery.

The fault rates can easily be converted into the mean time to defect by calculating the reciprocal. Fault rate data is also useful for predicting when an acceptable mean time to defect will be reached by using a software reliability model. This will provide guidance concerning the answer to the question of when to stop testing or when the consequences of failure no longer justifies the testing cost (Sherer, 1991).

Another useful metric or quality control technique is to keep track of critical bugs or 'Show Stoppers'. A 'Show Stopper' bug is a very serious bug that cannot remain in the product before being given to customers. 'Show Stoppers' must be fixed before the product development can continue to the next phase of testing. A product that has been thoroughly tested and contains no known bugs at time of customer delivery will usually exhibit excellent field quality. Unfortunately, today many software products are shipped with known bugs that are commonly documented in the product release notes. Our example phase metric for the testing phases is given below.

4. ***Test Fault Rate:*** This metric is defined as the number of faults discovered per time within each process testing phase for each product for each release.

7.2.2.5 Maintenance

The global metric Customer Change Requests has been previously defined as the number of change requests divided by the code size for the first year of field use. A technique for customer satisfaction survey is described in Chapter 14 to determine subjective measurements of customer opinion on a software product. It is desirable to monitor the rate of customer complaints over the life of a product. The number of complaints per time can provide insights into the acceptance of the product and provide indicators of when the product should be modified or replaced with a new product.

The customer complaint rate may be dependent on the number of units installed. Complex products may not exhibit certain bugs until the product is used by many users in different environments. Also one must be cautious reviewing fault rate data for very poor quality products. A small complaint rate may occur because the users have stopped using the product due to its poor quality. Our example phase metric for the maintenance phase is defined below.

5. ***Customer Complaint Rate:*** This metric is defined as the number of customer identified faults per time period from the time of first field use of the product through its lifetime.

An interesting study of the relationship between maintenance phase development productivity and McCabe's cyclomatic complexity measure is given in Gill (1991).

7.2.2.6 Example Summary

We have defined five example phase metrics to assist a new metrics practitioner with metrics definition. The examples are summarized in Table 7.3.

Table 7.3 Example Phase Metrics Summary

Metric	*Phase*	*Units*
Requirements Specification Change Requests	Requirements	No. Change Requests
Design Faults	HLD, Detail Design	No. Design Faults
Code Faults	Coding	No. Code Faults
Test Fault Rate	Engr., Syst., and Field Test	No. Faults per Time Period
Customer Complaint Rate	Maintenance	No. Faults per Time Period

7.2.3 Fault Detection

When faults are counted during the various software development process phases using the example metrics given above, it becomes possible to analyze the distribution of faults with respect to where faults are introduced and where they are detected. A fault detection stream example is given in Figure 7.4 (Möller, 1988). The top of the figure indicates the phases where faults are introduced. The bottom of the figure indicates how faults are discovered. An organization measuring for the first time may find that more than half of the faults are found during system test and field application.

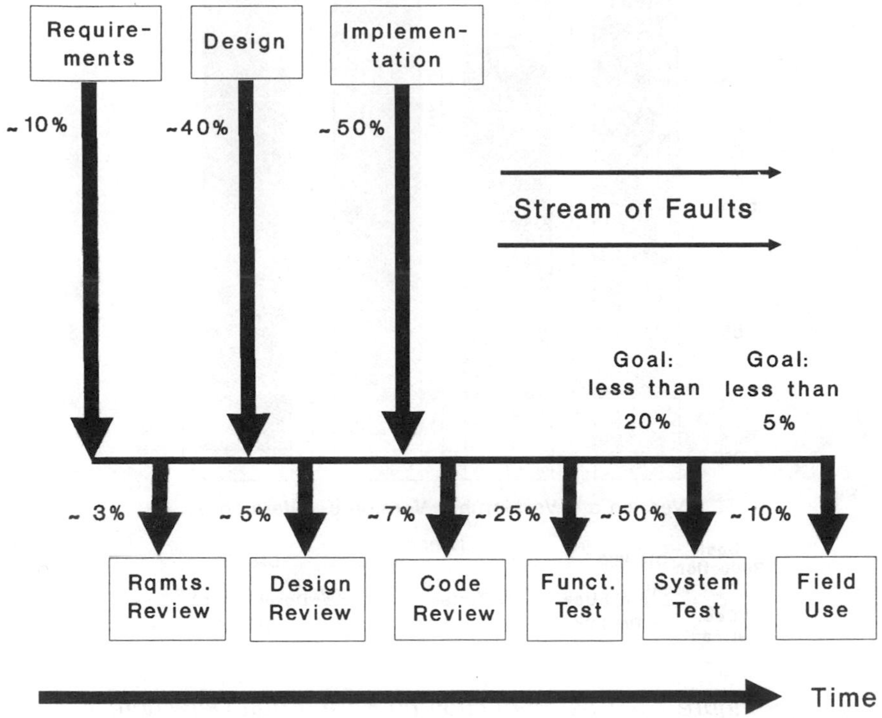

Figure 7.4 Fault Detection Stream.

It is highly desirable to identify and correct faults as early in the development process as possible. A realistic goal would be for less than 20% of the faults to be found in system test and less than 5% during field application. It is clear that as few faults as possible should be discovered by customers or users of the software system. In addition, the cost for correcting a fault increases for later phases of the development process. Figure 7.5 indicates the ongoing cost savings realized for a Siemens software product for multiple versions developed over several years. For this software environment the following costs per fault ranges within different phases were measured as indicated in Table 7.4.

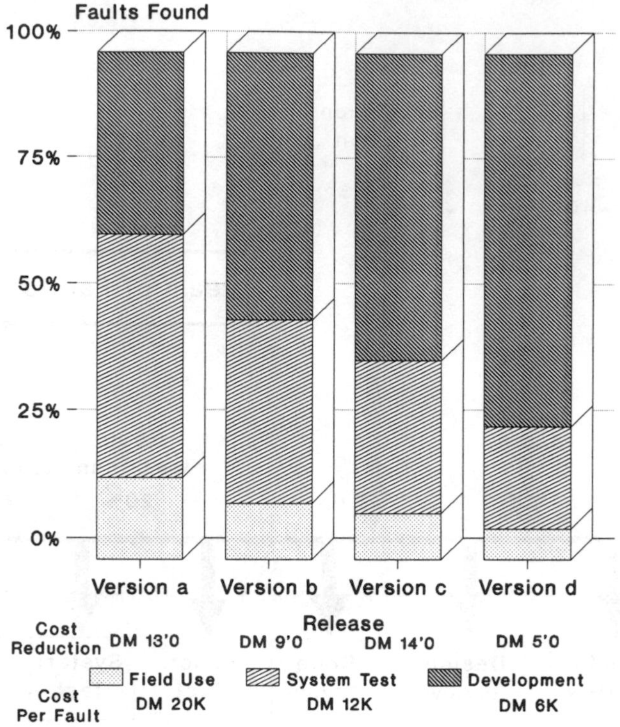

Figure 7.5 Cost Reduction by Early Fault Detection.

Table 7.4 Example Costs per Fault

Phase Where Found	*Cost Range (DM)*
Design Review	300-500
Development	3,000-30,000
System Test	6,000-60,000
Field	10,000-100,000

Thus it is more cost-effective to discover and correct faults as early in the software development process as possible. Of course there are additional savings to be made if faults are prevented and fewer faults are *introduced* into the product development process.

Another observation that has been made at Siemens is that the faults tend to be clustered within a small number of software modules. Empirical studies of multiple release products at Siemens indicate that approximately 50% of all errors are found in only 10% of the modified code. When these 'weak links' in the software system are identified, higher priority emphasis and resources can be applied to identify and correct as many faults as early as possible.

7.2.4 Fault Prediction

Once fault data is collected for a period of time, it may be possible to introduce fault prediction techniques into the project management process. Under certain ideal assumptions the curve of the sum of all faults already found is a saturation curve as given by a simplified representation in Figure 7.6 (Möller, 1988). In normal use this curve will contain 'ripples' at the phase boundaries introduced by new software releases and test resource allocation.

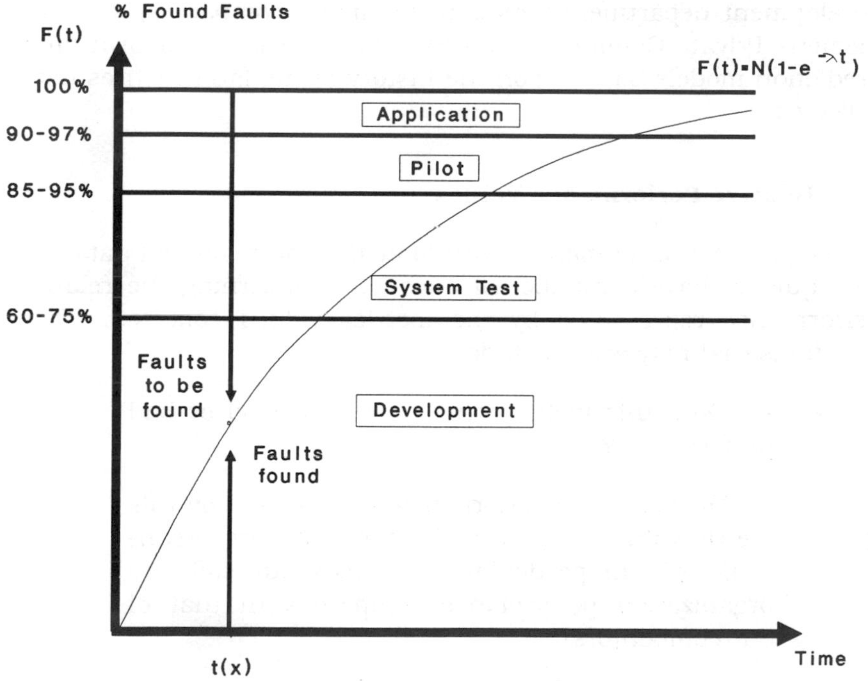

Figure 7.6 Faults Found at a Given Development Process Time.

The benefit of using a fault prediction model is that the fault detection rates can be compared with the predicted values to provide an indication of the current status of the software project. The fault prediction model can also be used to project the number of faults remaining in future phases of the development process. This may be useful for projecting resource requirements for more realistic business planning; e.g. what is the size of the software maintenance team necessary for support of a particular product?

There are a number of fault prediction models (Musa, 1987) and tools available to estimate the remaining faults in a software system. Examples of such fault prediction tools include SPQR/20 and Checkpoint provided by Software Productivity Research (SPR). These tools predict faults associated with requirements, design, code, documentation, and 'bad fixes'. In practice the predicted values will often vary significantly depending on the product application and environment. For example, the predicted fault values may depend on variables such as the programming language used, the rate of changed lines of code for a new release, software module sizes, and the expertise characteristics of the development department. As a result many companies, such as Siemens Private Communication Systems, develop their own fault prediction models based upon the history of the fault metrics data collected.

7.3 Relative Performance Values

A new practitioner of metrics with limited or no historical data will very quickly have a number of questions concerning the relative performance represented by the metrics values collected. The questions that may arise include:

- Does this metric value represent good or bad performance?

- How does the performance represented by this metric value compare with other software organizations? In particular, how does our software organization performance compare with that of our competitors?

- What are realistic goals for metrics that we can achieve?

An example of this situation occurred when writing this book. We were able to calculate that our book development productivity metric value was 1.58 Pages per Staff-Day. However, since our historical data is limited, we don't know if the productivity value represents good productivity or not so good productivity for writing books.

The new metrics practitioner can attempt to answer these questions by using commercially available tools which contain a data base of metrics from many prior projects. In this manner one may compare the metrics of a specific project with a composite 'average' software project. Many of these tools will subdivide the data base for comparisons among projects with similar product applications. Care must be exercised in making these comparisons because of differences in the definitions of the metrics; e.g. how a line of code is defined. The fault prediction tools are usually part of a software cost estimator package which predicts other software project management metrics such as schedule, resource loading, and development cost. Although these tools usually have a number of questions to tune the model to the specific development environment used, the primary input is the projected number of lines of code to be developed.

Many companies develop a set of 'rules of thumb' for determining good metric value performance and setting goals. These 'rules of thumb' are developed by a combination of comparing project performance within the organization over time, the use of tools containing data from other projects, and carefully trading metrics data with similar organizations.

In practice the sharing of metrics data among similar organizations in different companies is limited because many companies consider metrics such as productivity and fault rate data as company proprietary. It is often difficult for a company to divulge fault rate data which implies that their products are not perfect and contain bugs.

Although there is insufficient information available for good comparisons of relative performance when using metrics with limited history, Table 7.5 provides some 'rules of thumb' derived from Siemens projects for embedded, system, and communications software. The table gives typical values for the global metrics Productivity and Customer Change Requests. The size numbers (NLOC) are given in terms of the product size as defined by the Lines of Code global metric, while the Productivity and Customer Change Requests values are calculated by using the delta lines of code (DLOC), which is the number of lines of code that were added or modified for a current release as compared with the prior release. For a new product with its first release, the NLOC and DLOC values are equivalent.

Table 7.5 Typical Metrics Performance Values

Size (KNLOC)	*Productivity (DLOC/SD)*	*Customer Change Requests (Faults/KDLOC)*
2000	5	1.6
1500	7	1.5
1000	10	1.2
500	17	0.9
200	25	0.4
100	35	0.3

8 Tools

8.1 Introduction

When considering tools suitable for supporting software metrics, one comes to a paradoxical situation:

- on one hand there are plenty of commercially available tools for software metrics;

- on the other hand, many leading practitioners use home-made tools.

One reason is that many of the commercially available tools are code analyzers, which measure coding phase metrics such as Halstead's (Halstead, 1977), or McCabe's (McCabe, 1976) metrics, and not the global indicators used by leading-edge practitioners for software project management.

The reasons for this situation are mostly historical and reflect the evolution of the software industry towards metrication during the last ten years:

- initial over-enthusiasm in code metrics;

- disappointment with those metrics resulting in a backward step in metrication practice;

- emergence of a new wave of metrication practitioners which relies on global indicators such as those listed in Chapter 7 of this book.

There is currently a gap between the needs of these new wave practitioners and the tools available on the market. Unfortunately, limited commercially available tools exist that are optimally usable for this purpose.

Tools must be chosen or developed which support the software development process. They must be maintained and updated as the software development process is changed as a result of improvements. It is not recommended that tools be purchased, and then the development process is created or modified to match the tool.

However, tools support is necessary, and much help can be gained from the use of small tools developed on commercially available personal computer data bases or spreadsheets. This is the path followed by many of the leading-edge practitioners when developing their own tools.

The remainder of this chapter indicates desired functionality of tools for metrication. The aim is to provide some guidance for the implementation of such tools on commercially available packages running on a desktop computer. Whenever applicable, it will also state the advantages that can be obtained from commercially available tools.

It consists of three sections which correspond to the three categories of metrics described in Chapter 6:

- size
- product quality
- process quality.

The final part of this section is a synthesis of practical solutions for implementing tools in a simple way.

8.2 Communication Between Tools

A very important consideration to be taken into account when reviewing metrication support tools is that these basic metrics are not independent. Time (calendar or project), effort, and size play a very specific role as they are often used for normalizing purposes. Tools should therefore communicate, or at least share data on the same basic files.

In this respect, manual or poorly designed automatic transfer of files should be avoided. This is an extremely important consideration, and overly sophisticated tools are often a big problem in this respect, due to their intricate proprietary (and often undocumented) internal data format.

When designing home-made tools, the following rules should be considered :

i. only use widespread commercially available packages;

ii. always require the ability of these tools to process files produced by other tools, and in particular standard ASCII files;

iii. always require the ability of these tools to output files that can be processed by other tools, and in particular standard ASCII files;

iv. give preference to the spreadsheet for easy-to-use and isolated tools;

v. prototype all the tools on spreadsheets for validation;

vi. give preference to the data base with a programmable environment for an integrated metrics program at the business enterprise level.

8.3 Measuring Size

In Section 7.1.1, two example methods for measuring software size are given:

- lines of code (LOC) of various types
- function points.

These two techniques are further considered below.

8.3.1 Measuring Size by Counting Lines of Code

Multiple definitions exist for the basic unit of lines of code (LOC), and its most common multiple the 'kilo-LOC' or 'KLOC'. Lines of code can be counted with or without comments, including or excluding declarations, before or after incorporation of 'includes', with or without expansion of 'macros', and with many other variations.

This is further complicated when, for maintenance purposes, differential (or delta) lines of code are used. Furthermore, related units, such as number of statements, or number of instructions, are also sometimes used for size measurements and deleted code may also be counted.

The choice of a suitable definition of the LOC is typically a company choice. The choice in itself is not that important; however, the definition should not vary if one wants to establish references to compare projects.

This lack of standardization results in making size measurements by counting lines of code more complex than desired, and is one reason why this metric is not included in the tools which ought to provide it; e.g. editors, compilers, and configuration management tools.

The practitioner will then be left with designing and implementing his own LOC counting tool. This consideration should be taken into account when choosing the 'Company LOC'. In this respect, an easy-to-measure definition of the LOC should be preferred to a more sophisticated one which could require a more complex counting tool.

There are many ways to design LOC counting tools, and they need not be complex. As size of code is a common denominator, or normalizing metric for many other metrics, the LOC counting tool should deliver data usable by other metrics tools.

As the most common support for all these tools are either spreadsheets and/or data bases, the files produced by the LOC counting tools should be easily and automatically usable by these tools.

8.3.2 Measuring Size by Counting Function Points

There are a limited number of commercially available tools for counting function points. Tools could be purchased or developed to calculate the number of function points from source code. More ideally, function points could be calculated from requirements or design specifications prior to the existence of code. Some tools have been developed for deriving function points from well-defined specifications (e.g. military systems), and from design-level data.

8.4 Measuring Product Quality

The PYRAMID example metrics for software product quality are global indicators, namely 'system test faults' and 'customer change requests' (Subsection 7.1.2). Faults can also be counted at other selected points within the software development life-cycle (e.g. Design Specification Faults). Fault detection and correction as early as possible in the software development process is desirable. Rules for counting faults must be established; e.g. duplicates, major versus minor severity, etc.

The conclusion as to the commercial availability of support tools is immediate: there are no known tools to perform these measurements. In particular, code analyzers, which only produce low-level code metrics, are not applicable in this case.

The only practical solution is to design your own tools. Fortunately, this is fairly easy due to the availability of sophisticated spreadsheet or data base packages at low cost.

8.4.1 System Test Faults

For this case, one must record the number of faults discovered during system test. For safety critical products, this test is likely to be performed independently of the development (e.g. Independent Verification and Validation).

From the quality assurance point of view, System Test is one of the most important activities in software engineering. In particular, tracking the nature and origin of faults is an important aspect, as this will lead to development process enhancement. In this respect, when such a quality assurance system exists, 'System Test Faults' as a metric will just appear as a side product of the quality assurance system.

In this case, this metric will be collected in the same way, and by the same tools, as the fault reports. When this is done by automated means, or at least in electronic form, a small interfacing tool to convert data formats to the ones used by the spreadsheet or data base managing the metrics program might be necessary. Anyhow, automated tools should be preferred, and when collection is manual, entry in a spreadsheet/data base system suitable for further processing should be preferred.

When no fault-reporting system exists, implementation of this metric is a good way to introduce fault reporting. In this case, spreadsheets should again be used, at least for prototyping, and they should be configured in a way enabling:

- further processing of the captured data

- extensions to fault classification and corrective action logging and processing.

8.4.2 Customer Change Requests

Here again, for this type of metric, no common commercial tool exists. However, the problem of tools support is made more complex, since customer change requests may not be normally reported to developers, but to a product support department.

In this case also, the existence of a comprehensive quality assurance organization within the company will be a great support for implementing this metric.

A common task of a quality assurance department is to keep records of customer change requests (and/or complaints). This is used in the same way as our proposed metric; i.e., for effectively assessing the quality level of the products, with a view to enhancing the production process for better quality. In this case, organizational links exist between the product support and quality assurance departments, and some means of transferring information probably also exists. For obvious reasons, the 'Customer Change Requests' metric should be implemented using these existing information channels.

Since the basic number of customer change requests is to be normalized by code size before turning into a calculated metric, some relation must be established with the size measuring tool (LOC or function point counters). This might not always be easy, since the product support department might use a totally different data processing system than quality assurance. This is where the possibility to process plain ASCII files by the selected spreadsheet/data base system used for metrics implementation finds its utility; otherwise, a small interfacing tool will have to be designed.

When the quality assurance organization in the company is not formally in touch with product support, this is a good opportunity to establish this valuable link. However, this may be difficult since organizational links will need to be established.

8.5 Measuring Process Quality

Here again, there exists no common commercially available tool that directly fulfils our needs. However, conventional project management tools will prove very useful for calculating the two example metrics (Subsection 7.1.3). These two metrics, 'Schedule', and 'Productivity' are separately addressed below.

8.5.1 Schedule

This metric might be the one for which existing project management tools will prove most useful as they keep track of planned, and actual work time. The only additional operation required to derive the metric is the ratio between the two.

This can be accomplished in numerous ways. The decisive criteria for the choice of tools is their ability to interface and exploit the files of the project management tool.

Two cases can be distinguished, depending on the prior existence of a project management tool:

- when such a tool exists, a small interfacing tool is likely to be designed to interface between the spreadsheet and/or data base used to implement the metrics;
- when no such tool exists, the choice between various commercial brands should take into account the ease of processing its data files.

8.5.2 Productivity

Here again, a project management tool will be a major help in establishing this metric and the same considerations as above concerning its choice apply.

The ease of communication plays a major role in the choice of tools as this metric is directly derived from exploitation of data provided by:

- a size measuring tool
- a project management tool.

It may also be possible to obtain the data necessary for metrics calculation from existing corporate cost accounting systems. Systems which collect effort and cost data for the tasks performed by individuals within the development group are good sources of data for productivity calculations and other related metrics.

8.6 Synthesis of Usable Solutions

Figure 8.1 indicates the data flow between various tools used to implement the five global example metrics described in Section 7.1. This highlights the necessity of easy communication and interchange of data between the tools.

Table 8.1 indicates various applicable solutions. The first column lists the five global example metrics, the second column indicates commercially available tools when applicable, while the three last columns respectively address the use of home-made, spreadsheet, and data base tools.

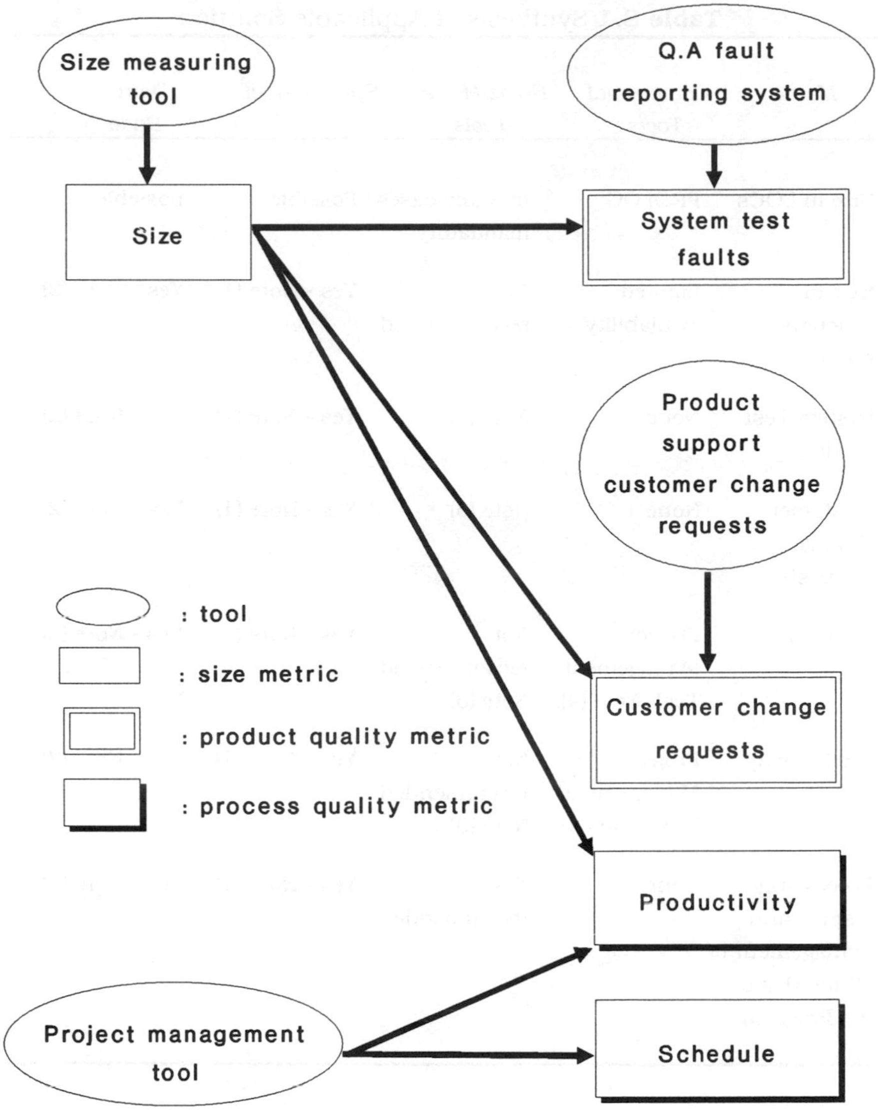

Figure 8.1 Data Flow Between Metrics Support Tools.

Table 8.1 Synthesis of Applicable Solutions

Metric	*Commercial Tools*	*Home-Made Tools*	*Spreadsheet*	*Data Base*
Size in LOCs	PROLOC	In many cases mandatory	Possible	possible
Size in function points	Limited availability	Not recommended	Yes - Note (1)	Yes - Note (2)
System Test Faults	None	Note (3)	Yes - Note (1)	Yes - Note (2)
Customer Change Requests	None	Note (3)	Yes - Note (1)	Yes - Note (2)
Schedule	Project Management Tool Note (4)	Not recommended Note (3)	Yes - Note (1)	Yes - Note (2)
Productivity	Project Management Tool Note (4)	Not recommended Note (3)	Yes - Note (1)	Yes - Note (2)
Processing, display and management of all metrics of the Program	None	Not recommended	Yes - Note (1)	Yes - Note (2)

Note (1) : spreadsheets are recommended for prototyping and validation and for departmental metrics programs.

Note (2) : data bases are more suitable for company-wide programs.

Note (3) : a small interfacing tool might, however, be necessary.

Note (4) : Project management tools will not directly give this metric. However, they provide necessary basic data for its calculation.

In conclusion, it is possible to state that ease of data interface should be the main criterion when choosing any tool for metrication support purposes. This is true both for:

- the tools to be used for processing the metrics;

- but also, whenever possible for the tools providing basic data such as :

  . quality assurance fault reporting system;

  . product support customer change request processing system;

  . project management tool.

When considering all the elements, the recommended solutions to generate, store, manage and display the global example metrics are:

- spreadsheet for prototyping, and a departmental Metrics Program;

- data base with programmable interface for a larger scale Metrics Program.

9 Best Practices and Benefits Experience - Siemens

9.1 Siemens Nixdorf Systems Software

9.1.1 Application Overview

This section documents the best practices used for systems software development within Siemens Nixdorf Informationssysteme AG (SNI). SNI was formed in October 1990 by the merger of the Data and Information Systems Group of Siemens AG and Nixdorf AG. The practices described herein currently represent a merging of the best practices of the two companies. In particular, many of the practices described were initially implemented within Siemens systems software development projects approximately eight years prior to the merger with Nixdorf. As a result, we believe that this application of software metrics may be one of the earliest applications found in Europe. The practices that are described give examples of global metrics applied to software business management.

Systems software refers to software that is developed for controlling the utilization of general-purpose computer systems. It includes software such as operating systems, computer language compilers, data base management software, utilities, and data communications software. The primary operating systems developed and maintained are BS2000, which is an operating system that runs on Siemens mainframes, and SINIX™, which is a Siemens supported version of the UNIX™ operating system.

The software products developed range in size from approximately 10,000 lines of code for small utility applications to more than 5 million lines of code for a complex operating system. Computer languages that are primarily used are C, SPL, and

Assembler.

There are approximately 3000 software engineers and support specialists involved in developing and maintaining these system software products. Many of the developers are located in the Munich and Paderborn areas in Germany, although there are development centers located around the world. Some of the larger satellite development centers in Europe are located in Namur, Belgium and Vienna, Austria.

9.1.2 Development Process

The SNI systems software development process is documented in a Methodology Handbook. The handbook contains *what* must be done for developing software products in approximately eighty pages of text and diagrams. Detailed procedures, standards, and training material augment the handbook describing *how* the process should be implemented. The steps described are obligatory for systems software development projects. Software project managers can add more stringent requirements and additional milestones for a specific project. The process also allows to some extent an overlap of the sequential process steps.

The SNI software development process has been defined in order to plan and develop products within a fixed schedule and cost framework, so that customer acceptance and satisfaction is maximized. The process is made up of phases within which certain defined actions or process steps must be executed. Each phase has a fixed start- and end-point called a milestone. Milestones are decision points at which the phase just completed is critically examined to determine the project status and initiate any corrective actions which may be necessary. This is accomplished by quality assurance actions which take place in all project phases. These actions have priority over other development activities, since it is recognized that the later in the process that errors are identified, the more costly is their correction.

The SNI software development process consists of four phases spanning the entire life-cycle of software development activities. The phases and major process steps are given below.

Process Phase	**Process Step**
Planning & High-Level Design	Requirements Study
	Solution Study
	Functional Design
	Interface Design
	Detailed Project Plan
Detailed Design & Implementation	Component Design
	Code Design
	Coding
	Component Test
	Functional Test
Quality Control	Product Test
	System Test
Installation & Maintenance	Pilot Installation & Test
	Customer Installation

Between phases, project responsibility passes from the control of one organizational group to another, and there are formal handoff/acceptance procedures which are executed.

A Technical Product Controller is responsible for the implementation of the product requirements by the systems software development organizations or contractor. A Marketing Product Controller is responsible for the definition and evaluation of the product requirements. The Marketing Product Controller is the primary interface to customer organizations which will distribute the product to users. A Product Development Committee is led by the Technical Product Controller for the purpose of managing the product development plans and activities.

9.1.3 Metrics Used

The metrics (called *Kennzahlen*) measure the quality of SNI products, and the productivity and profitability of the software development and maintenance process. The results of measurements for current development projects provide indications of actions required to keep a project on plan. The results of measurements for completed projects accumulate to a wealth of empirical knowledge. This experience is useful for estimating development costs, the expected volume of defects for new projects, and for improving the development process.

The following primary data are needed for calculating the software metrics.

- Problem reports and defects counted during Implementation (after first successful compilation), during Quality Control (Product and System Test), during Pilot Test, during the first year after Customer Installation, and total. Within SNI Systems Software *defects* are defined as problem reports that have been approved as real faults. In this manner misunderstandings, duplicates, etc., are excluded from the count of defects.

- Development costs in Deutsche Marks (DM) and Staff-Months.

- Maintenance costs in DM.

- Turnover (Sales) in DM.

- Product size in gross lines of code (BLOC), net lines of code without comments and blank lines (NLOC), and newly developed or changed net lines of code as compared to a prior release (DLOC). These lines of code counts are determined by code-counting tools.

9.1.3.1 Quality Metrics

The following metrics are defined for calculating product quality.

- **QKZ1** = The number of defects counted during Code Review, Component and Functional Test divided by the number of thousands of lines of code (KDLOC).

- **QKZ2** = The number of defects counted during Quality Control divided by KDLOC.

- **QKZ3** = The number of defects counted during Pilot Test divided by KDLOC.

- **QKZ4** = The number of defects counted during the first year after Customer Installation divided by KDLOC.

- **QKZ5** = The total number of defects received per fiscal year from the field after Customer Installation divided by the number of KNLOC for the latest version in the field.

- **QKZ6** = The total number of field problem reports received after Customer Installation divided by the number of defects identified for every fiscal year for each product line.

- **QKZ7** = The total number of defects received per fiscal year from the field after Customer Installation divided by half the sum of KDLOC delivered within two years.

- **QKZ8** = The number of defects counted after Customer Installation divided by the total gross number of delivered lines of code (KBLOC) by fiscal year for each product profit group and for the overall system software development organization.

9.1.3.2 Productivity Metrics

The following metrics are defined for measuring development team productivity.

- **PKZ1** = The development costs divided by KDLOC.

- **PKZ3** = The maintenance costs divided by the number of defects after Customer Delivery for every fiscal year and for each product line.

- **PKZ4** = The total gross lines of code (KBLOC) delivered to customers divided by the total Staff-Months expended for system software development for every fiscal year.

- **PKZ5** = KDLOC divided by the development effort in Staff-Months.

- **PKZ6** = KDLOC divided by the development time in months.

9.1.3.3 Profitability Metrics

The following are metrics for calculating software business profitability.

- **WKZ1** = Turnover in DM divided by the software development costs in DM for every fiscal year for each product line.

- **WKZ3** = Turnover in DM divided by the total costs for development, maintenance, and marketing for every fiscal year for each product line.

9.1.4 Quality Improvement Techniques

Some of the activities successfully applied at Siemens Nixdorf Systems Software to improve the development process and consequently the quality of software products are summarized below.

- ***Quality - The Most Important Factor for Success.*** In 1980 the top management of the newly formed Systems Software Division set up its global goals: develop systems software with outstanding quality, on time, and with minimal cost to reach high customer acceptance as the basis for business success. This explicitly stated global goal, with quality as the first priority, was identified at a time when quality was not yet seen as the most important factor for a software business.

- **Quality Deputy.** Management focus on quality is reinforced by the identification of a high-level manager as the *quality deputy*. This highly visible position reports directly to the top business manager of SNI Systems Software. Among other responsibilities, he is in charge of initiating and controlling activities to improve process and product quality. The quality deputy also participates in a company-wide SNI Quality Committee which coordinates all activities and procedures necessary for process and product quality improvement.

- **Quality First.** The focus on quality is commonly expressed with two slogans. They are regularly cited in speeches by management during various seminars. They are also made visible using quality posters. These two slogans are:

    - ***'Quality before Deadline before Functionality'.*** Project plans must be as accurate as possible. On the basis of many years of experience, a high percentage of systems software projects reach the expected goals. But when problems do arise, quality has the highest priority. The quality level must not be reduced.

    - ***'Quality from the Beginning'.*** The development process is defined and steadily refined in order to avoid defects. For those defects which do occur, efforts are made to identify and correct them as early as possible, and to avoid them in the future.

- **Reviews.** The development process model described in Section 9.1.2 is defined as a result-oriented model. The result of every process step, be it a study, a test specification, or code, must be reviewed for quality assurance with one of the following techniques:

    - **Development Document Control (DDC).** The DDC is a written review process which is particularly suited to requirements studies, solution studies, and functional designs. For each document submitted for DDC, the Technical Product Controller selects a 'Referee'. The Referee selects experts and other interested staff as 'Reviewers'. The Reviewers are requested to find errors and weaknesses in the document. The Referee functions as an arbitrating authority to resolve differences of opinion between the reviewers and author.

    - **Formal Inspections.** They are compulsory for newly developed and changed code after the first clean compilation; i.e., before the use of automated testing. They are also well suited to replace DDC inspections of documents within early process steps, but they have not yet been frequently applied. The formal inspection technique incorporates the use of an oral review, and the recording of data and actions resulting from this review (Fagan, 1976). The tally lists used for counting and categorizing defects are the basis for defect prevention activities and one input to calculate quality metrics. The technique of formal inspection has been introduced through a comprehensive internal training program.

- **Quality Reporting.** Metrics data are regularly reported to management. The internal publication which receives the highest management attention is the annual quality report. It contains textual and graphical summary data for the overall system software business as well as for specific product lines. It contains the metrics data for the completed fiscal year plus the prior several years. In this manner the progress of quality and productivity improvements are highly visible. For project-controlling purposes the full-year time interval is too long. Thus a reduced quality report is also published in the middle of the year. Additionally, statistics such as those concerning open defects or quality costs are reported to management weekly or monthly. The management interest and attention that these reports receive result in corrective actions when necessary, and further general actions for process improvement. Summaries of the metrics progress for the past several years, and the goals for the new year are periodically reported to all employees using the employee newsletter and employee meetings.

- **Qualification.** 'Quality from the Beginning' is also applied to the selection and training of people. Only software developers with a high-level of qualification and education are hired. When they begin employment, they are trained on SNI Systems Software products and the software development process. In this way new software staff members quickly come up to speed and adapt to the successful software development culture. Regular training and workshops are used to keep staff knowledge up-to-date.

- **Motivation.** Training and workshops, especially on product development process and methodology, are used as one way to help motivate people to concentrate on the quality of their work. Increased awareness of the importance of quality is also reached through quality audits. For a particular project the conformance to the defined general process, the application of certain methods, the use of tools, and the conformance to standards such as documentation standards are reviewed and discussed. In addition there are also performance incentives. Every year one development group, a team of about four to eight developers, receives a so-called Q-Oscar together with an award. For exceptional technical achievement, every year a developer is allowed to attend an international overseas conference. The trip may be prolonged for a short vacation. Also every year innovation projects are defined which help the development teams to reach extraordinarily challenging business or technical goals.

- **Component Ownership.** A technique that SNI uses oriented towards software maintenance is the identification of individuals with responsibility for each software component. The purpose is to ensure that technical knowledge of a component is preserved beyond the lifetime of individual projects. The responsibilities of the component owner are:

  - Acquiring, retaining, and documenting *detailed technical knowledge* of the product component.

  - *Technical responsibility* for maintenance activities on the product component.

  - Conducting or managing *maintenance implementation* on the component.

9.1.5 Benefits

Some of the benefits that were observed as a result of the Metrics Program are summarized below.

- **Improved Quality Culture.** The incorporation of metrics within the Methodology Handbook and the emphasis on improved product development process and training, have resulted in a business culture where quality is important. In particular, the Annual Quality Report raises the visibility of progress trends such that supportive management actions can be implemented.

- **Better Process and Product Quality.** Having process and product quality data for the past eight years, and annually publishing the last five years of data, raises the visibility of the substantial improvements that have been achieved. Although specific metrics having to do with defect rates and such are considered company proprietary, the overall trend towards higher quality products as a result of process improvements is an impressive business accomplishment.

- **Improved Customer Satisfaction.** The techniques described herein have resulted in improved customer satisfaction - both for users and internal customers. This satisfaction can be inferred from quantitative data concerning defects discovered by customers such as the trend of the QKZ8 metric, and from customer opinion surveys.

- **Model for Other Siemens Businesses.** The successful application of quantitative methods at SNI has created a model for other Siemens businesses. The long history of application of these techniques and the depth of expertise within SNI have inspired other Siemens businesses to implement similar Metrics Programs. Although the types of software products developed may be much different from systems software, the general concepts and improvement techniques apply to other businesses. Many Siemens businesses have taken the concepts developed by SNI, and modified them for their own specific environment and quality improvement goals. This approach has resulted in development methodology handbooks written for other Siemens software-intensive businesses located throughout the world.

- **Business Growth and Profitability.** The most important benefit of the quality improvement activities at SNI has been continued successful growth of sales and profit margins. SNI today is considered a very competitive business enterprise and a primary vendor of computer systems in Europe. This success probably would not have been achieved without a continual commitment to quality with incremental process improvements over many years.

9.2 Siemens Nixdorf Application Software

9.2.1 Application Overview

In addition to systems software, Siemens Nixdorf develops application specific software. These software products can be application specific standard products (e.g. software tools, CAD, banking, office automation, transportation) or custom application software. Custom application software is developed to meet the needs of a single customer. This software is specially developed or adapted by customizing standard products or other existing custom application software. The application software can be developed and delivered as part of a customer system which also includes hardware, system software, and possibly customer support and training.

The application software products are quite diverse depending on the specific requirements. Applications may be developed in a variety of computer languages (e.g. C, C++, FORTRAN, COBOL), and they range in size from approximately 10 KLOC to 4 MLOC.

Approximately 3000 software developers are located in design centers throughout the world. Many of the developers are located in Munich, with other large centers in Paderborn, Frankfurt, Berlin, Barcelona, and New Delhi.

9.2.2 Development (Master) Process

The Siemens Nixdorf applications software development process is called the 'master process'. With such a wide range of applications and product sizes, the process gives general guidelines that must be augmented dependent upon specific customer requirements. Specific projects can be initiated at different milestones within the master process dependent on the type of customer order received (e.g. customer system, product development using a customer-supplied functional specification, adapting or porting of an existing product). The master process is documented in a Process Engineering Handbook which has been periodically updated since its introduction in the early 1980s.

The master process is illustrated in Figure 9.1 and is divided into four process segments:

- Problem Analysis
- Product Definition
- Implementation Engineering
- Maintenance/Operation.

Each process segment is subdivided into a number of process steps, each of which is delimited by milestones. Depending on the size and type of project, process steps can be combined or refined into greater detail. Decisions are made concerning whether the project should continue to the next step at the completion of certain project-important process steps. These reviews are called end-of-phase decisions.

Process Segment	*Process Step*
Problem Analysis ↓	Statement of Problem Initial Situation Analysis Problem Space Spec.
Product Definition ↓	User Requirements Detailed Func. Specs. Global Implement. Specs.
Implementation Engr. ↓	Detailed Implement. Spec. Component Specs. Tested Components Integrated Product Alpha Tested Prod. Accepted Prod.
Maintenance/ Operation	General Product Release End of Maintenance

Figure 9.1 Master Process.

9.2.3 Project Control and Monitoring

Project control and monitoring begins with the development of a project plan at the initiation of the project. The project plan contains the following as well as other information:

- product structure
- project work structure
- staffing plan
- schedule
- project organization
- quality assurance mechanisms
- precautions against risks
- outsourced subproducts.

The project environment contains a number of support and decision-making functions. Independent Technical and Business (Financial) Controllers (TC, BC) are assigned to the project to monitor product and process quality. In addition to quality reporting, they provide assessment and recommendations for the end-of-phase decisions. The Technical and Business Controllers have independent reporting relationships from the Project Manager and the Decision-Maker. The Decision-Maker is usually the Project Manager's Supervisor; he is the authorized representative to the customer. The Controllers provide recommendations to the Decision-Maker concerning the quality and financial assessment of the project.

Unlike project status review meetings, phase review meetings do not involve the discussion or solution of problems or the distribution of general information. Rather, the end-of-phase decision meeting purpose is to decide whether the project should proceed to the next process step. The end-of-phase decision includes an evaluation of the quality assurance process.

The internal general project structure is shown in Figure 9.2. Dependent on the size of the project, various support services as shown are provided to the Project Manager.

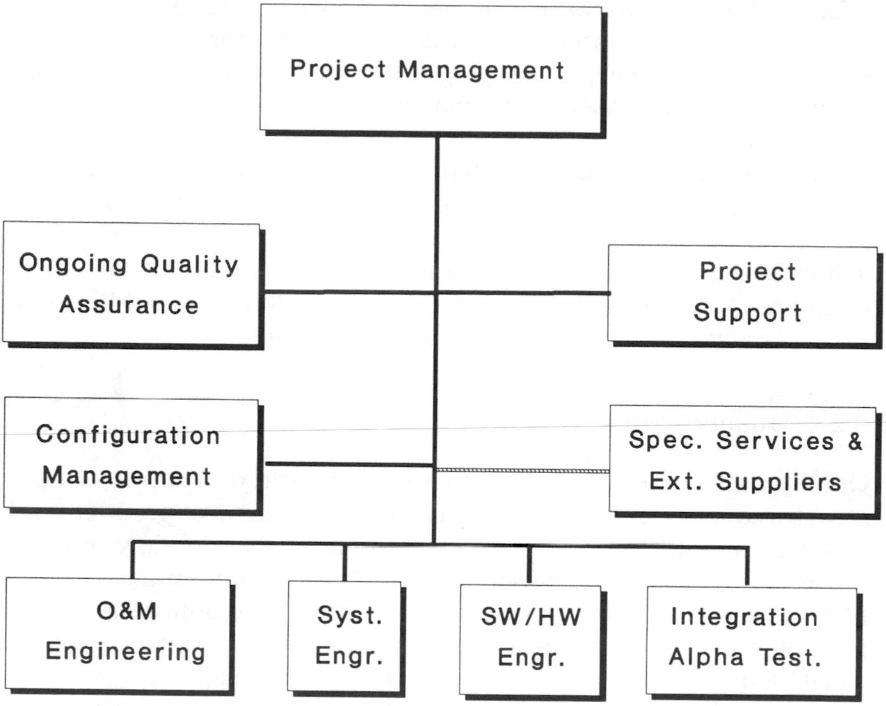

Figure 9.2 Internal Project Structure.

Preliminary costing is performed after the project structure has been determined. Effort estimates are made for each work package. The following information is estimated:

- Size (e.g. pages of documentation, KLOC for each work package)
- Manpower Requirements
- Other Resources (e.g. CPU time).

Experienced personnel and prior metric data are exploited from earlier similar projects for determining the new project effort. After effort estimation has been completed, project costs are calculated by applying cost rates per staff-hour, and then adding any surcharges. As the project progresses, costs are monitored and compared to the baseline estimates which are contained in the project plan.

The metrics that are reported by project management include planned versus actual milestone results, planned versus actual product quality assessment values, fault statistics for the different software development phases, and planned versus actual costs. Graphical tools for project status communication include Milestone Trend Analysis and Cost Trend Analysis diagrams.

9.2.4 Quality Assurance

Quality assurance refers to all measures required in terms of both structured and operational organization to ensure product and process quality within the application software development process. At SNI, the functions which generate quality in the projects are organizationally separate from the monitoring of this process by Controllers. It is the task of the Controllers to provide constructive criticism during the product development process. Controllers have no executive authority in the product development process; their suggestions are communicated and acted upon through quality reporting.

Quality reporting is implemented via phase appraisals and project reports. Quality cost metrics and metrics concerning the occurrence of faults are periodically compiled together in the *'Q-Spiegel'*. This document is a bulletin to inform management of the overall quality situation concerning application software at SNI. It also becomes a handy reference document which captures corporate experience with metrics data.

9.2.5 Quality Assessment

By looking at quality as 'fitness for use', it can be described by sets of characteristics representing different aspects of this fitness. Therefore the quality of products, processes, and documents is assessed using such sets (Figure 9.3), that completely covers the respective quality aspects. For product quality, the set complies with ISO 9126.

Not all of the characteristics are measurable by using quantitative scales. Thus, lists of criteria are provided for each of the characteristics. While the criteria may vary depending on the process step for which the assessment applies, the criteria lists are dedicated to the respective steps. Depending on the satisfaction of the criteria, quality is assessed using a standard four-level scale (O - no deficiencies, L - minor deficiencies, S - serious deficiencies, A - fatal deficiencies).

The advantage of this methodology is its application to all aspects of quality independently of whether quantitative measures are available or not.

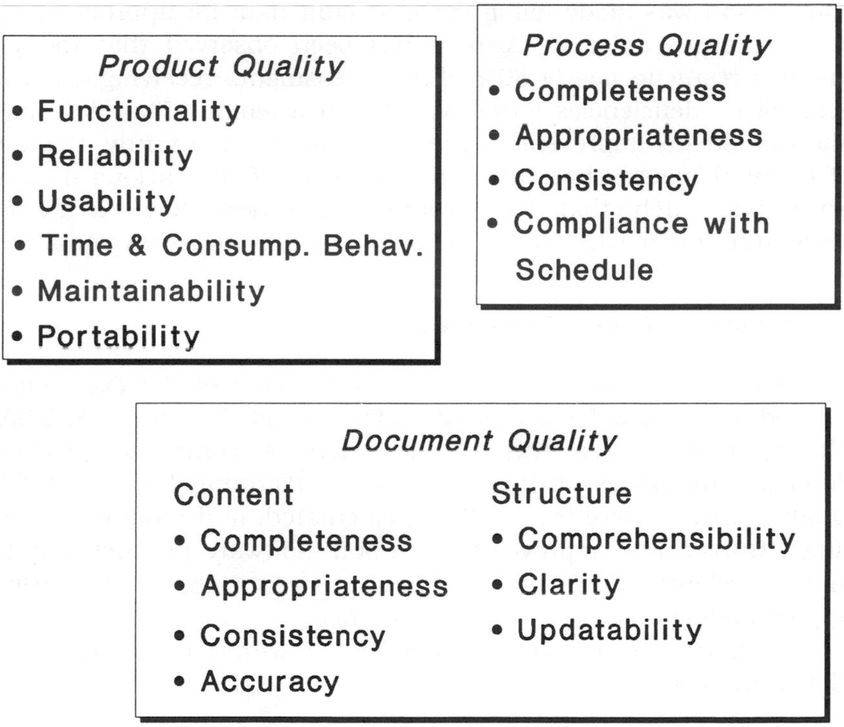

Figure 9.3 Quality Characteristics.

9.2.6 Benefits

The benefits of the master process and use of metrics has resulted in substantial quality improvements over time. By describing the quality of products and processes, distinctive quality targets can be stipulated more precisely, and deficiencies can be recognized earlier and more reliably. The public distribution of quality assessments within the organization helps motivate developers to avoid deficiencies arising from carelessness within the development process. It also encourages discussion and, if necessary, correction of the quality assessments. The quality improvements can be observed by comparing the current metrics data in the Q-Spiegel with earlier versions. For example, as a result of the application of these techniques, faults reported by customers have been reduced to approximately one-third of prior levels. This comparison was made using the field fault data for approximately 100 assessed projects. Also, it has been observed that today's projects result in nearly 80% of all assessments receiving a grade scale of no deficiencies found at the first attempt. This data has shown a steady improvement over time. More importantly, the use of nominal metrics has raised the visibility of the various quality attributes, such that the product developers have a better understanding of what actions should be taken to improve quality.

9.3 Siemens Medical Electronics

This section reviews the practices and benefits of the experience learned at Siemens Medical Electronics, Inc. in Danvers, MA, USA. The approach taken was to implement a controlled product development process called the Product Planning Process (PPP). Quality metrics were then defined, calculated, and monitored over time. Substantial improvements in both software product quality and development team productivity were observed during approximately a three-year period of time.

The metrics and approaches used fall within the category of global metrics.

9.3.1 Product Application Overview

Siemens Medical Electronics (SME) designs, develops, and manufactures patient-monitoring systems for use in hospitals throughout the world. The patient-monitoring products are typically used in Intensive Care Units, Cardiac Care Units, and Operating Rooms within hospitals.

Approximately twenty product development teams are developing patient-monitoring products depending on the application of the device in the hospital (e.g. bedside monitors, central nurse's station, recorders, displays). The devices utilize microprocessor-based hardware platforms using Motorola and Intel processors, and they utilize real-time operating systems. The devices are connected within the hospital for real-time data collection and distribution using a proprietary local area network.

The code is written primarily in C with some assembly language code for time-critical applications. The software development environments used include Sun Microsystems workstations, personal computers, and VAX minicomputers running SunOS, MSDOS, and VMS respectively.

High quality code is required in order to provide customer satisfaction and to ensure patient safety. To increase software quality, emphasis has been put on increased development methodology with carefully controlled specifications and reviews, better testing procedures and tools, and the use of quality metrics to measure progress. The products developed and production process techniques utilized are regulated by the US Food and Drug Administration. The best practices described, as well as similar practices applied to the hardware development process, represent a number of activities associated with overall company efforts to increase Preproduction Quality Assurance (Food and Drug Administration, 1989).

9.3.2 Product Planning Process

The SME Product Planning Process (PPP) is a methodology for coordinating activities involved with product development. It ensures that business and product development objectives are consistent. It addresses the entire life-cycle of a product from Research to Post-Production Support. The PPP increases product quality by controlling the development process, and performing reviews during the various product development phases. The review flow used for the PPP is given in Figure 9.4.

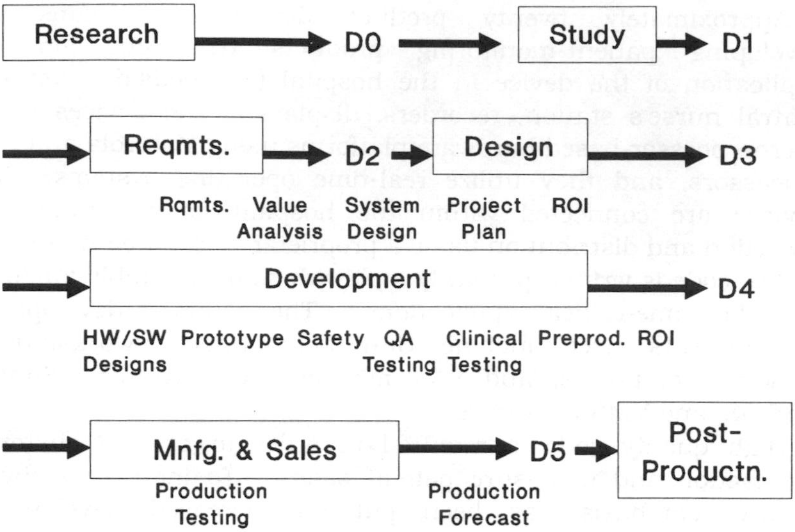

Figure 9.4 Product Planning Process Review Flow.

A Decision Board makes business and funding decisions between the various phases of the PPP. A Product Control Group (PCG) is established to be responsible for the progress of the development activities. Representatives from all functional departments (e.g. Marketing, Research & Development, Manufacturing) are members of a PCG. The goal is to coordinate, anticipate, and identify parallel activities for all departments that are involved with product development. This approach is often referred to as 'Simultaneous Engineering'; the goal is to maximize product quality and reduce development time (Dumaine, 1989; Gordon, 1989; Schmelzer, 1989). The working relationships of the PCGs and the Decision Board are given in Figure 9.5.

The activities within the PPP for improving software quality are summarized in Figure 9.6. Reviews, testing, and metrics are implemented during the various activities associated with software design and development.

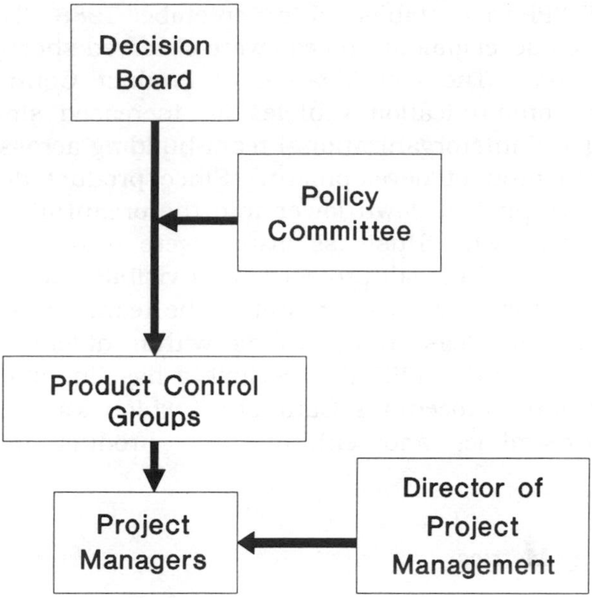

Figure 9.5 Product Planning Process Management Control.

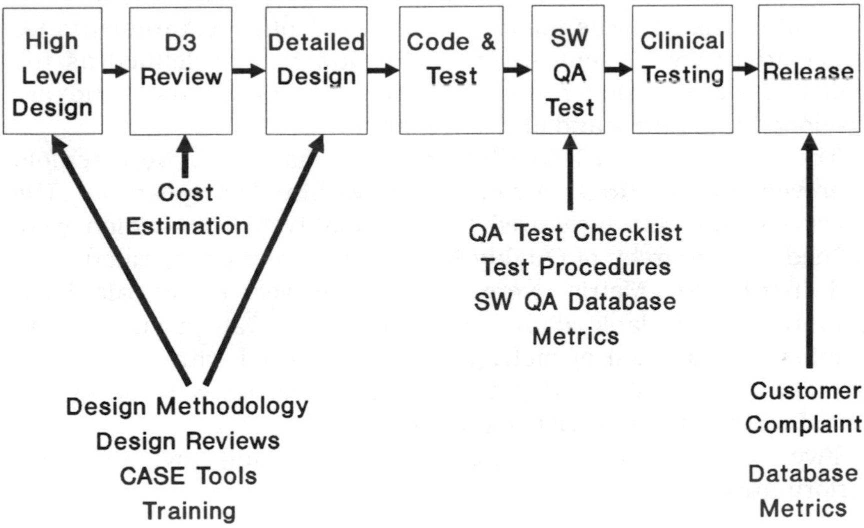

Figure 9.6 Software Quality Improvement Activities.

The SME PPP was established in September 1988. The benefits of a controlled development process were observed shortly after the implementation. The identification of Product Control Groups created the communication vehicles for increased simultaneous engineering and interorganizational team-building across functions involved with product development. Since product development decisions were pushed down lower into the organization, product ownership increased. Business issues were resolved in a more timely manner, and overall project status visibility was increased. Product quality improved as a result of the team approach which brought together ideas from experts within different technical disciplines. The initial PPP also became a baseline starting point for the corporate 'Procedures Committee' which was chartered to improve, streamline, and enhance the product development process.

9.3.3 Quality Metrics

Subsequent to the initiation of the PPP, an R&D Quality Metrics Program was started to measure the progress of the various activities for improving quality and development team productivity. The program began with a definition of R&D Quality, improvement goals, and identification of the internal customers. A survey of internal customers was made in order to identify requirements for anticipated improvement areas. R&D Quality was defined as the ability to develop better products, that are fit for use, and are developed in a timely and efficient manner.

The goal of the R&D Quality Program was to achieve a tenfold improvement of R&D performance within five years. The improvements were measured by the Quality Metrics which were defined. A hierarchy of Quality Metrics was developed, calculated, and distributed. Metrics were defined that were easily calculated from readily available data. Each function was given a small number (five or less) of metrics to be concerned with in order to increase the visibility of key metrics. New metrics were developed and abandoned as experience increased.

Five metrics were defined for measuring overall R&D performance.

> ***S-Measure:*** This is a measure of development schedule adherence comparing the achieved schedule with the project plan reviewed at the

beginning of the development phase.

> ***C-Measure:*** This is a measure of customer complaint activity in units of complaints per thousand units installed.

> ***M-Measure:*** This is a measure of Mean-Time-Between-Failures of device hardware.

The B-Measure and D-Measure are software quality metrics. The calculation approach for these measures is given below.

> ***B-Measure:*** This measure is calculated by dividing the total number of software problems reported by the Quality Assurance (QA) function during the product validation testing divided by the number of thousand lines of delivered source code for each product for each release. The B-Measure is an indicator of the software quality and testing effectiveness of the softwarc engineering function responsible for the product.

> ***D-Measure:*** This measure is calculated by dividing the number of change requests made by customers for the first year of field use of a given release by the number of thousand lines of delivered source code for that release. This is a measure of prerelease testing and overall software product quality.

The application of the above software quality metrics to the development activities as defined by the Product Planning Process is illustrated in Figure 9.7. Additional software quality metrics that were defined and monitored include the number of problems found during development and clinical testing, the number of QA and clinical test versions required before release, and the number of known and projected problems at the time of release.

A consistent Software Metrics Program provides the benefit of increasing the visibility of the software development process. Software engineering personnel improve their performance when it is measurable. The data collected is archived and available to Project Managers who must plan future product developments. With better estimates of projected product development activity and quality, the business decisions that are made concerning the profit opportunities for alternate products become more realistic.

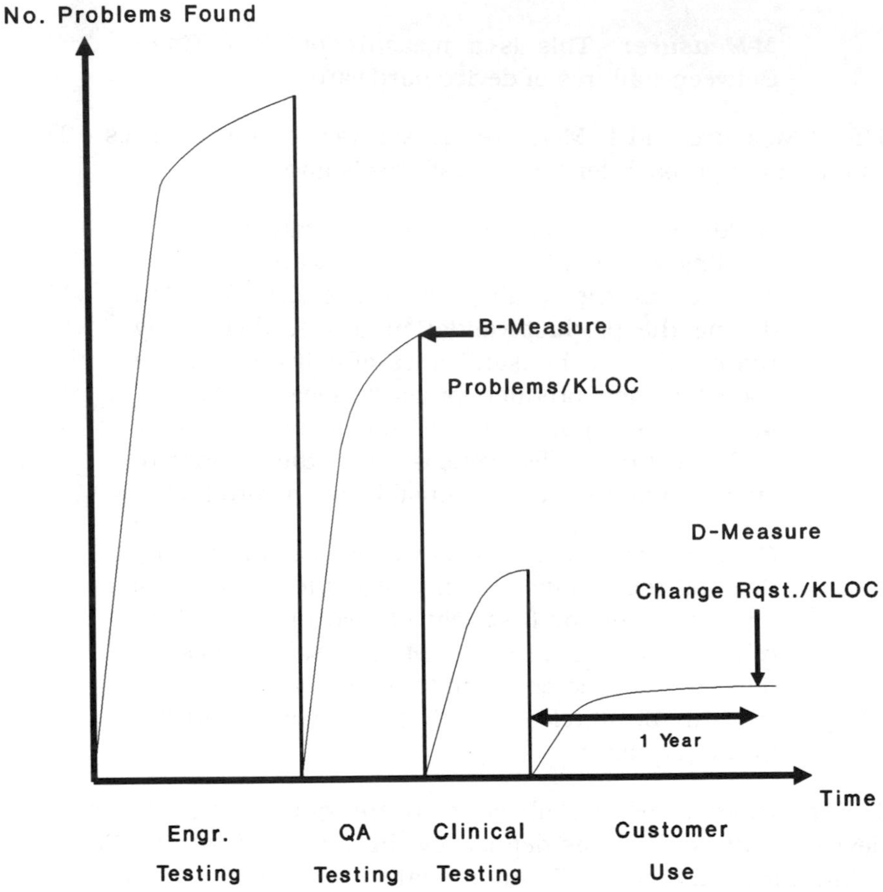

Figure 9.7 Software Quality Metrics applied to the Development Process.

9.3.4 Quality Improvement Techniques

Some of the techniques that were applied at Siemens Medical Electronics for improving software quality are summarized below.

9.3.4.1 Data Bases

The data used for metrics calculation was taken from existing data bases. These data bases included the QA Test Data Base which recorded software problems that were detected during Validation Testing, and the Customer Complaint Data Base which recorded complaints made by users of equipment installed in the field. The existence and control of the Customer Complaint Data Base were required by FDA regulations.

9.3.4.2 Code-Counting Tool

A code-counting tool called PROLOC was ported to the SME development environment. This provided a simple consistent approach to obtaining lines of code values for different projects and products which was used as a complexity normalization factor for the calculation of the metrics. The PROLOC tool provides a Siemens standard method for counting lines of code for a large number of programming languages. It also provides the capability to compare two software releases for counting changed and added lines of code. Prior to the use of this tool, different projects counted code using different techniques. These differences resulted in much confusion when cost estimation tools were applied and productivity calculations were made comparing various projects.

9.3.4.3 Validation Testing as a Controlled Bottleneck

A Software QA Validation Testing function was established to identify measures of software quality through formal functional testing. The function was set up such that every product release was required to undergo testing prior to in-hospital clinical testing. This very quickly resulted in better more consistent quality across the products, since products with unacceptable quality (determined by the B-Measure and the severity of problems found) were modified and resubmitted for validation. The visibility of the testing function also became very high because no product could proceed to clinical testing without having been submitted to validation testing.

9.3.4.4 QA Test Checklist

A Software QA Test Checklist was developed to be used as a test plan and communication vehicle between Validation Testing and Software Engineering. It specified the tests that should be conducted on a given release, what types of system configurations should be tested, the individuals responsible for reviewing and approving test results, and special instructions such as the order of tests to be performed.

9.3.4.5 Video-Taping of Problems

A practice that was successfully utilized by the Validation Testing Function was to video-tape the sequence of actions associated with creating the characteristics of a specific bug. This was a time-saving communication aid useful in describing the problem to Software Engineering so that it could be quickly reproduced and corrected. This was especially useful during system stress-testing during which the testers were encouraged to deviate from the written test procedures based upon their experience from breaking prior systems.

9.3.4.6 Media Verification

The Validation Testing Function provided a service to the company for verifying the Master Media that would be released to Manufacturing for duplication and distribution in large quantities. In this manner there was high confidence established that the software released was the software that was tested, and that it was properly built and loaded onto the Master Media.

9.3.4.7 Document Control

Good document version control is required for software product development. In addition to code version control, it is necessary to control the versions of Requirements Specifications and Test Procedures. The existing Engineering Change Order (ECO) Procedure which was used to control manufacturing and hardware design documentation was used for this purpose. Also, software releases were controlled by ECO, and test results were archived with the released software.

9.3.4.8 Software Version Naming Standard

A standard was developed for naming and labelling of software versions. The standard was set up such that the software quality of the specific software version was encoded within the name. For example, 'X' was used to indicate that the software was controlled within Engineering, and that it was only to be used for test purposes. A 'D' indicated that the software could be used to demonstrate product characteristics, but the quality level was not acceptable for patient use. The letter 'T' indicated that the software passed Validation Testing, and its purpose was restricted to Clinical Testing. The letter 'V' indicated the highest quality level in that the product passed all testing, and it was available for customer use.

9.3.4.9 Decision Board Metrics Review

It became a practice to present and review metrics data as part of the PPP Decision Board Reviews which were held between Project Phases. For example, at the end of the Development Phase and prior to the Manufacturing Phase (D4 Review), metrics data for Validation and Clinical Testing were reviewed. As a point of interest, the process required that the release of a product for manufacturing and sales was authorized by the SME President.

9.3.4.10 Monthly Reports

It became a practice to summarize key metrics in a published Monthly Management Report. This not only served the purpose of increasing the visibility of the metrics, but it also became a handy reference document as a source of data for going back in time to compare current metrics values with past values.

9.3.4.11 Schedule Commitment Uncertainty

A practice that was introduced to the organization was the use of schedule/cost uncertainties coupled to the PPP Phases. The S-Measure used the schedule presented at the D3 Review as the baseline schedule for calculation. By the time of that review, the Requirements Specification and the High-Level Design Specification were complete. According to Boehm (Boehm, 1981), at that point in the life-cycle, the software estimate should be accurate to within a factor of 1.25. It was felt that a good Software Project Manager could successfully manage this uncertainty level, perhaps through a combination of team casual overtime or weekend effort. Thus the schedule presented at the D3 Review was viewed as an organizational commitment made by the Project Manager and supported by R&D Management. Conversely, schedules given prior to the D3 Review were viewed as estimates with a high degree of uncertainty. For example, schedules proposed prior to the existence of a Requirements Specification could exhibit an uncertainty factor of two or more (Boehm, 1981).

9.3.5 Benefits

Some of the benefits that were observed as a result of the Metrics Program are summarized below.

9.3.5.1 Improved Quality

Software product quality was observed to improve subsequent to the initiation of the improvement activities and metrics. The attitude was established that every release should exhibit better quality metrics than the prior release, and that each new project should utilize better quality practices than existing projects. The hope was that every engineer would do a higher quality job each day as compared to the prior day. The metric data supported the improvement observation. For example, the B-Measure exhibited a 35-fold improvement and the D-Measure exhibited a six-fold improvement, as measured by comparing the current releases with the initial measured releases across different projects. The qualitative sense that software quality was improving was also validated through employee surveys.

The improvement achieved in product quality for the B- and D-Measures is illustrated in Figures 9.8 and 9.9 respectively. The nomenclature used is that projects are labelled with the letter 'P'. The second letter indicates the relative time-frame of the project. Thus project 'PB' was initiated after project 'PA', and most likely has utilized an improved software development process. Releases are labelled with the letter 'R'. Successive releases are indicated by the second number; thus release 'R2' for project 'PA' occurred later than release 'R1'. Although the data presented was collected for a limited time-frame (2-3 years), the trend towards lower defect rates provided encouragement that the improvement techniques that were implemented were having a positive influence on software product quality.

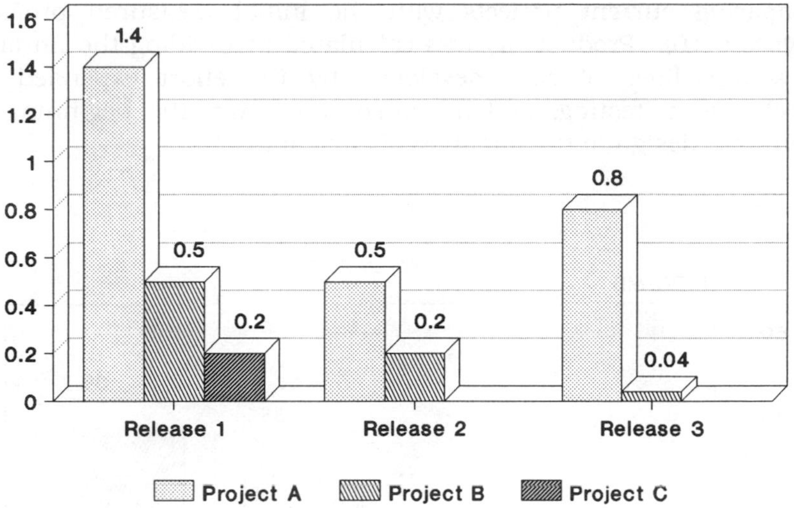

Figure 9.8 B-Measure Values (Faults/KLOC).

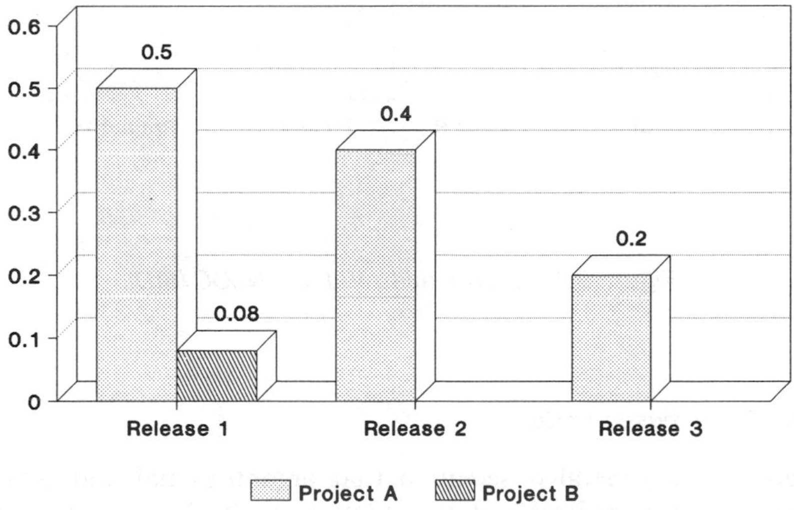

Figure 9.9 D-Measure Values (Change Requests/KLOC).

9.3.5.2 Improved Productivity

Software development team productivity was observed to improve across different projects. The improvement measured was two-fold comparing current projects with the initial measured projects (Figure 9.10). Productivity was calculated by dividing the number of source lines of code developed by the effort expended by development, testing, and documentation from the beginning of high-level design to the initiation of clinical testing.

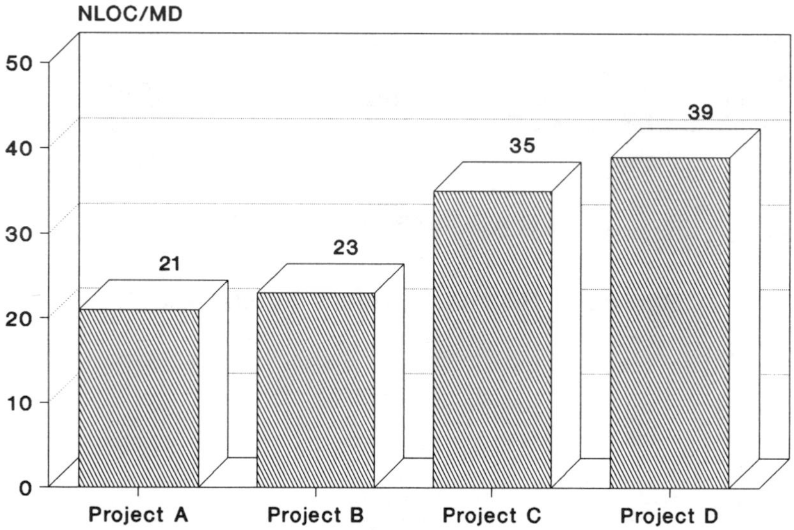

Figure 9.10 Productivity Values (NLOC/MD).

9.3.5.3 Increased Pride

There was a general observation that organizational and project pride increased subsequent to initiation of the Metrics Program. Engineers are trained to solve problems. For software engineers assigned to fault-correction tasks, an attitude often develops that the product they are working on is poor quality as a result of the many faults that they directly observe. The existence of metrics provided the ability to compare the quality levels attained with published data on the quality of other software products. The metrics also indicated progress in improving quality levels throughout the software life-cycle. This resulted in a realization by many software engineers that although they were exposed to many faults, correction of the faults was part of the development process, and that on a relative basis the product quality was quite good. This feeling was culminated when the company was selected to participate in an industry survey of software development practices within 'excellent' projects. A description of the development process techniques used for this project is given in Section 9.4.

9.3.5.4 Better Business Decisions

The metrics provided an input to management to make better business decisions. For example, if the customer complaint metric data indicated that a product was exhibiting lower quality as compared with other products, perhaps this product was a candidate for replacement. Management could then make the decision to form a new project team with the charter of replacing the existing product with a better, higher quality one.

9.3.5.5 Improved Staff Motivation

The Metrics Program indirectly contributed to better staff motivation. The metrics helped to quantify what was expected for a project team to do a good job. This provided guidance to individual engineers with respect to which of their personal activities would be appreciated, and what should be given high priority. The product development process also helped contribute to the definition of job functions across the various organizations. A training program was also established as part of the quality improvement activities in order to improve staff skills.

9.3.5.6 Improvements Basis

The metrics were a contributor to identifying which quality improvement activities should be initiated. It was observed that one could not improve the product development process until a process existed, albeit an imperfect one. The metrics were an indicator of where the potentially best return-on-investments would be achieved for quality improvement efforts. The metrics also were a tracking tool to indicate which quality improvement activities were having a positive impact on the organization.

9.3.5.7 Common Terminology

The metrics and their definitions as well as the PPP helped establish a common terminology within the company. This was an aid to communication, particularly across different functional organizations (e.g. Marketing/Engineering). This common terminology helped create a corporate culture in which there was high value given to quality improvement.

9.3.5.8 Improved Team Cooperation

The metrics indirectly helped improve the attitudes of personnel with respect to the degree of cooperation provided within the PCGs, Quality Improvement Teams, and Project Development Teams. When the metrics helped to quantify the severity of a quality problem, it is much easier to motivate the people assigned to fix that problem to work together towards a solution. It became obvious that a joint goal across functional organizations was higher quality products.

9.4 S700 Patient Monitor Project Assessment

9.4.1 Product Application Overview

The S700 is a small-sized patient monitoring system developed by Siemens Medical Electronics. The development process and application of metrics for this product resulted in a very high quality software system. The number of Customer Change Requests per KLOC measured during the first year of customer use was less than 0.1. This equates to less than ten software faults found during the first year of field use for approximately 1000 units installed during that time.

The S700 is a family of patient monitors (Figure 9.11) used within hospital Intensive Care Units, Cardiac Care Units, and Operating Rooms. The monitors interface to a proprietary local area network for intrahospital communications, alarm annunciation, and display. The software functionality (206 KLOC) is used to process, analyze, and display real-time signals originating from sensors attached to the patient. The monitor measures and provides alarms on physiological variables such as ECG, respiration, temperature, and blood pressure. Substantial software is also implemented to provide a user interface (primarily used by nurses), which utilizes touch-screen inputs (Figure 9.12).

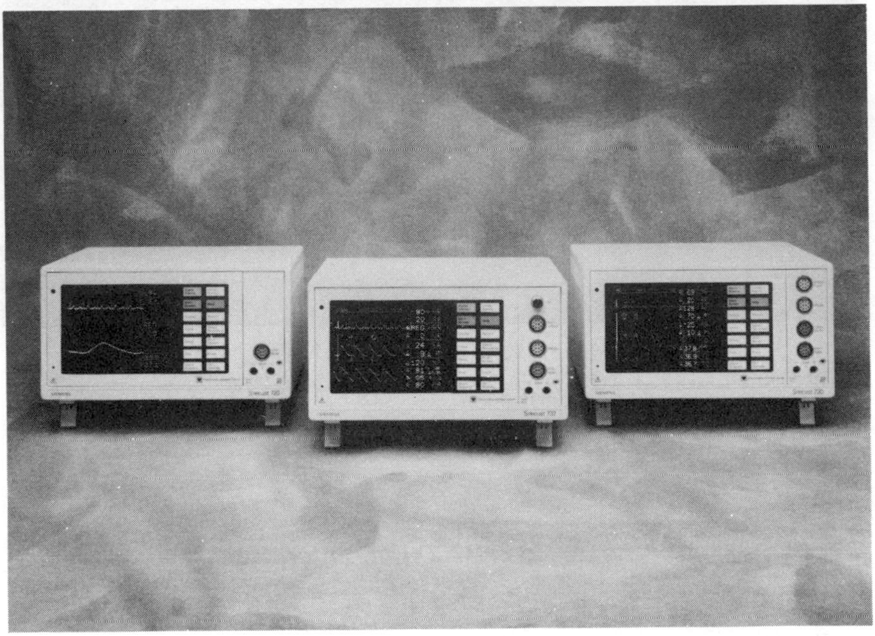

Figure 9.11 S700 Patient Monitor Family.

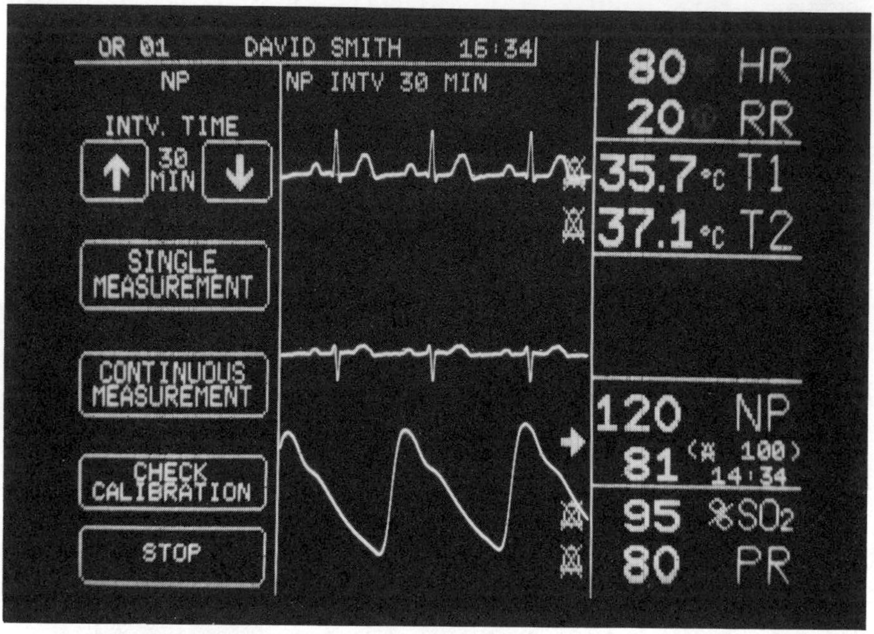

Figure 9.12 S700 User Interface.

Preliminary requirements, project planning, and high-level design work were initiated in early 1987, and a basic engineering prototype was developed and demonstrated in August 1987. The development team was expanded in early 1988 to prepare the first software release for field testing in the fall of 1988. Four major software releases were made between January 1989 and September 1990, each providing additional functionality. In May of 1990, the development team staffing was reduced from a peak of fourteen to a four-person staffing level.

9.4.2 Software Measures and Practices Study

In 1990, Software Quality Engineering (SQE) and Xerox Corporation initiated a study to benchmark the software development practices and metrics used by world-class companies (Hetzel, 1990). The study was conducted through survey questionnaires and site visits. An industry baseline was established, and then ten 'excellent' projects were selected for detailed benchmarking and comparison. In addition to Xerox and Siemens, the other companies that participated in the benchmarking study were IBM, AT&T, GTE, NCR, and Dupont. The S700 Project was the Siemens project that was included in the detailed benchmarking and comparison of the ten software projects. The SQE assessment team made a site visit to Siemens on October 21-22, 1990, and conducted interviews with the development team.

The survey report authors concluded that the industrial application of metrics was very immature and much less established than other areas of software development methodology. They concluded that less than 10% of the companies surveyed were applying metrics with varying degrees of success. Furthermore, as a result of analyzing the ten 'excellent' projects, they concluded that good measurements are an essential element and prerequisite to effective software engineering management.

As compared to the other software projects that were benchmarked by SQE, the S700 project had the highest rank scores on both parts of the survey. This was a strong positive reinforcement for the Metrics and Quality Improvement Programs that were introduced at Siemens Medical Electronics several years earlier.

9.4.3 Development Process

A structured product planning process was used for the S700 Project with defined phases and management reviews. A Product Control Group was established with representation from multiple functions including personnel in Germany where the hardware design and production facility were located. Emphasis was placed on very careful development of the software requirements and design specifications. Tight control and progress reporting was maintained throughout the project.

The functional requirements and high-level design specifications were carefully reviewed, maintained, and updated. Design reviews were performed informally, but were taken very seriously with active participation by the team members. Unit test was also informal, and it was the responsibility of the engineer who developed the code for that unit. Integration testing was done by the entire team, and faults were recorded and tracked. Test procedures were developed in parallel with the software with the help of the QA test organization. The tests were run by the development team before the system was delivered to the QA test organization for validation testing. The tests were rerun by QA as part of the formal validation testing, and stress testing was also performed by QA.

The development team had a high priority goal from the beginning of the project to provide a fault free system to the QA test function on schedule. It was also a high priority goal to ship software to customers with no known software bugs. The project team faced tight schedule constraints and pressures, and substantial casual overtime was expended.

The emphasis on high quality code with no known faults was a major contributor to the excellent field product quality that was subsequently measured.

9.4.4 Metrics Practices

The schedule adherence metric was closely monitored. Weekly status tracking reports were generated and monitored using a PC-based project data base. The reports indicated the effort expended for each person against work breakdown tasks, and an updated forecast of effort for completion. The effect of these reports was that remaining effort was forecasted weekly such that potential schedule slips could be predicted and mid-course corrections could be made.

The work items were developed after high-level design, and then stored in the project data base. The data base contained information concerning task effort required and expended, priority, assigned individual, and estimated and actual lines of code. The major milestones and accomplishments were reported to management monthly with an issues list and resolution plan, and an updated project schedule.

Lines of code were estimated during the high-level design phase, and used as an input to the COSTAR PC-based tool (Softstar Systems) which provides schedule and cost estimates based on the

COCOMO Model (Boehm, 1981). The PROLOC tool was used to measure lines of code for each release and module. The tool measures delivered, changed, deleted, and added lines of code as compared to the previous release. As each software module was completed, the size was measured and compared to the original estimate.

Faults were recorded and tracked from integration testing through field use in data bases maintained by the project team and QA. The fault data was used to calculate the global quality metrics for software defined in Section 9.3.3.

9.4.5 Observed Positive Influences on Quality

The SQE Assessment Team made a number of observations concerning the positive influences that led to the success of the S700 Project. The primary influences were the emphasis on quality (fault-free) software, the up-front planning, requirements, definition, and design, and a close-knit talented development team. These observations are summarized below.

- **Quality Emphasis.** Quality was considered important from the beginning of the project. This attitude spread to all functions, and attracted high quality staff to the project.

- **Weekly Progress Metrics.** The work breakdown structure was developed and maintained weekly. Progress and effort remaining were measured weekly and every month were summarized for management review.

- **Requirements & Design Emphasis.** Much effort and time was expended up front to produce good functional requirements and high-level design specifications.

- **Specification Maintenance.** The functional requirements and high-level design specifications were maintained and updated throughout the product development.

- **Team Effort.** The project team formed close-knit relationships and worked well as a group; for example, when everyone would perform testing when a new integration build was made. Team spirit was cultivated also through non-work-related social functions such as volleyball games and pizza parties.

- **Design Reviews.** Informal design reviews were conducted on all high-level design features and most of the low-level design features.

- **Architecture Control.** Design issues were identified and resolved through very frequent meetings of the team leaders. Good understanding and control of the system architecture were considered critical for project success.

- **Testing.** Testing was considered very important, and considerable effort was expended developing good test procedures. The engineering development team and QA worked effectively together to produce a thoroughly tested high quality product.

9.5 Siemens Private Communication Systems

9.5.1 Application Overview

Siemens Private Communication Systems designs, develops, and sells communication systems throughout the world. These systems are known as telephone switching systems, private telephone exchanges, and private branch exchanges (PBX). The Siemens products are called HICOM™ systems. The metrics that are described are examples of global metrics.

This Siemens business is made up of approximately 26,000 employees. Nearly 700,000 systems have been installed for 400,000 customers worldwide.

Approximately 800 employees in Europe are involved with software development. New software versions, depending on the application, typically take 1-2 years to develop. The product sizes are approximately 1-3 MLOC, and represent an investment of 100-300 staff-years to develop. Most of the code is written in CHILL, and a large part of it is shared among the various versions within a product line.

In addition to Europe, distribution and development activities in the United States are substantial having resulted through acquisitions of Tel-Plus Communications and mergers with Rolm Systems and the Rolm Company. Rolm Systems is involved with product development, and the Rolm Company is a joint venture with IBM for product sales and service primarily in North America. Major software development centers are located in Munich, Germany; Santa Clara, California; and Boca Raton, Florida.

9.5.2 Development Process

The Siemens Private Communication Systems software development process is documented within a Software Development Handbook. The handbook has been periodically improved and revised since first being used in 1982. The handbook states that software development must meet three fundamental requirements:

1. The software must achieve the required quality level.

2. It must be completed within the agreed schedule deadline.

3. The development must not exceed the estimated cost.

The handbook defines the development process results and environment. It identifies the framework within which a software development team proceeds in the course of a project. The consistent application of the development process has resulted in the establishment and consolidation of a 'software culture' with a common technical language, system of values, and customs for all those involved with software development.

The handbook provides a series of general guidelines for all development projects. Each project manager is expected to map the general guidelines to the particular project and supplement the process with project-specific procedures. Project-specific adaptations are primarily dependent on project size. For example, process phases may be combined for smaller projects.

The software development process is described by a series of process sections, phases, and subphases (Figure 9.13). Each (sub)phase is concluded with a milestone. A milestone is defined as a point in time within the development process at which:

- Specific (sub)phase requirements have been completed (e.g. specifications, source code, test reports, etc.).

- The (sub)phase results have been reviewed and approved by a quality assurance function (e.g. through design reviews, code inspections, test results, etc.).

- The (sub)phase results have been released, and they can be used for future (sub)phase activities.

The completion of a milestone must be explicitly determined, and recorded in the project documentation. A Phase Review meeting is required at the completion of System Design, Component Integration, and System Test. The other milestones may optionally have Phase Reviews depending on the project size, difficulty, and complexity.

The handbook also contains guidelines for project documents such as design specifications, code documentation headers, and test reports. A number of useful forms are also provided for documenting the results of design and code reviews, and test results.

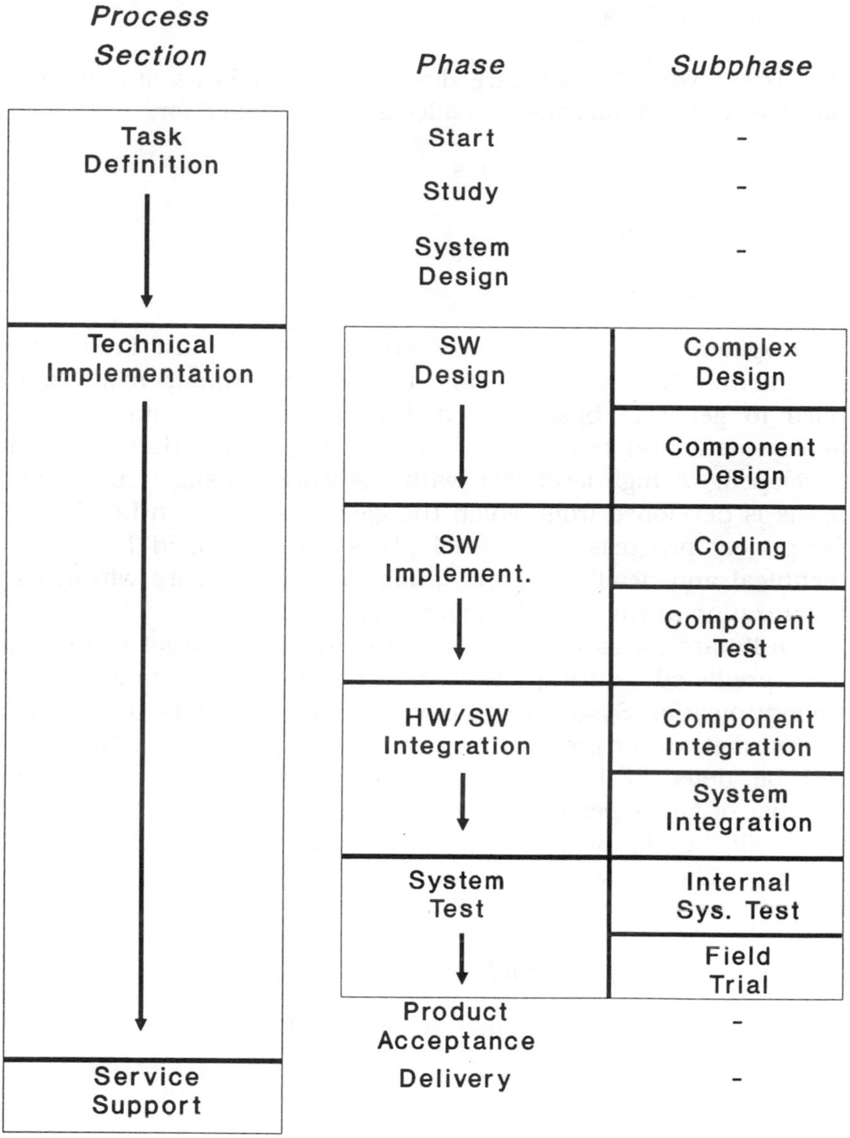

Figure 9.13 Software Development Process.

9.5.3 Metrics Used

Consistent with the software development goals as stated in the handbook, global metrics are collected and tracked for:

- Development Costs
- Schedule
- Faults.

Development schedule and costs are forecasted in the Project Plan document. The PC-based Time Line Project Management tool is used to generate baseline schedules, and to monitor schedule achievement and cost. Two levels of project schedule plans are developed. A high-level plan with the work packages and critical paths is developed from which the global metrics can be observed for project progress. Low-level plans are developed for internal technical and deadline coordination for each activity within each organization at each development site.

Faults are measured and compared with the target values that are predicted during System Design. Siemens Private Communication Systems has developed a model based upon past project metrics for predicting the number of faults per KDLOC that will be detected throughout the development. The predicted number of faults per KDLOC is given as a range of detected faults that will be discovered at different times of the development process. The phases where faults are measured and compared to the model include:

- Software Design
- Software Implementation and HW/SW Integration
- System Test
- One Year after Completion of System Test
- Remaining Field Problems after One Year.

In addition to comparing the number of faults detected during the various phases, targets are specified for the number of known and not yet corrected faults by priority class. For example, no known priority 1 faults can be in the system at the beginning of System Test or Product Acceptance.

9.5.4 Quality Improvement Techniques

9.5.4.1 Management Support

The Software Development Handbook contains a Preamble written by a high ranking executive. This Preamble establishes the support and interest of management. It briefly introduces the aims and uses of the Handbook. It states that the standard development process is an aid for helping to avoid errors during product development, or at least to detect them as early as possible.

It is stated that the handbook is a general target, which must be supplemented by the initiative and decisions of the project team. It does not replace close teamwork, which is based upon mutual trust, of the individuals involved with product development.

The Preamble states that development process technology must progress and adapt to changing requirements. Thus it is requested that feedback and suggestions be given to the handbook authors for integration into future editions.

9.5.4.2 Quality Assurance Plan

A Quality Assurance Plan is developed which contains the project-specific quality goals such as the milestone acceptance criteria, expected fault prediction and distribution, manpower assignments, required documentation, and test methods. An individual expert is identified to assist the project manager with all the tasks related to quality assurance. The basic definition of 'Quality' which is used is reproduced below.

> *Quality* is the entirety of features and characteristics of a product or of an activity that relates to the suitability of the product or activity to satisfy given requirements.

The management of quality assurance is decentralized. The quality expert is closely coupled to work with the project manager and development team. A small centralized Software Quality Assurance function acts as a corporate catalyst for training, tools, and techniques. It maintains and communicates 'best practices' information within Siemens Private Communication Systems. Critical tools are supported centrally where they are utilized within a transnational development environment.

9.5.4.3 Project Control

Project control functions are performed throughout the entire duration of the project, and they are intended to guarantee an orderly procedure as well as comply with the product quality, schedule, and cost metrics target goals. A Project Plan document is generated which contains the product development activities such as deadlines, milestones, costs, major effort tasks, and assignment of personnel and other resources.

The progress of the project is supervised, monitored, and controlled using information generated by:

- Regularly held status meetings
- Phase review and decision meetings
- Monthly project reports
- Quality reports.

Management emphasis is placed on schedule timing control rather than cost control. Experience at Siemens Private Communication Systems indicates that projects that meet their schedule milestones will usually meet their development cost budgets. These project control concepts are taught during workshops given for all project managers.

9.5.4.4 Phase Anticipation

It is suggested that some phases be anticipated as a means to reduce the risk associated with key design decisions. It is recognized that it is often extremely difficult to assess the consequences of a design decision. Therefore it is encouraged that future development phases be anticipated using such techniques as prototype development, more detailed specifications, trial implementations, etc. Furthermore, it is suggested that the anticipated activities be restricted to the minimum necessary to safeguard decisions, and that the current phase be completed as soon as the necessary results are available.

9.5.4.5 Configuration Management

Configuration management is aimed at controlling the process of change during the project. For this purpose it provides metrics, procedures, tools, and information. Examples of the types of project information that is controlled are:

- Change requests (Modification Requests - MRs)
- MR implementation decisions
- Source code
- Design and development documentation
- Product structure information
- Release information.

9.5.5 Benefits

9.5.5.1 Experience Data Base/Fault Prediction

The extensive amount of metrics data that Siemens Private Communication Systems has collected over many years enables it to maintain an experience data base. This data base is useful for comparing plans for new projects with data collected on prior projects.

The data base has also enabled the development of a fault prediction model based on metrics collected from past projects. This fault prediction model is tuned for the specific applications developed and the development process phases. This model predicts fault rates per KDLOC for the various phases both in terms of the number of faults that will be detected and the percentage of faults found in each phase. The QA approach for measuring these faults (e.g. review, test) is also specified. In this manner, current projects can monitor their fault rate metrics and compare it with the model throughout the software development process. Projects which do not conform to the model limits can be given additional management attention in order to anticipate potential project-related problems.

9.5.5.2 Design Control/Code Reuse

The handbook requires that a product structure plan be developed initially during the System Design Phase. This plan identifies the overall hierarchy of system functional units. The benefit of this document is that it serves as a basic communication vehicle for describing the functions and structure of the system to be implemented.

The product structure plan also helps to identify opportunities for code reuse. Since many products are developed with specialized functionality depending on the application, the reuse of core code is a major productivity enhancement benefit.

9.5.5.3 Fault Priorities and Acceptance Criteria

Four priority levels are defined for faults that are identified during development. During the test phases, a fault that stops the continuation of further development work (a 'Show Stopper') is given a high priority. For field trials, faults that have a negative impact on the customer are given a high priority. This system has the benefit of helping to guide decisions concerning resource allocation for problem correction.

The product quality acceptance criteria are also defined in terms of priority levels. In this manner, well-informed decisions can be made concerning which products have acceptable quality levels for proceeding to the next phase or ultimate customer use, or which products must be reworked.

9.5.5.4 Business Success

The practices described have been a major contributor to the business success of Siemens Private Communication Systems. The HICOM Systems have received numerous orders from customers throughout the world. In January 1989, the HICOM 300 System was the first ISDN communication system to receive approval for connection to the German public ISDN network. The ten-year emphasis on software development process, quality, and metrics has been a success factor for developing quality products that are desired by Siemens customers.

9.6 Siemens Automation

9.6.1 Application Overview

Siemens Automation develops factory automation systems products for applications such as Computer Integrated Manufacturing (CIM). Approximately 20,000 people are employed worldwide by this Siemens business. The business headquarters is located in Nürnberg, Germany, with larger facilities also located in France, Austria, India, and the United States.

This section describes the experience of a part of Siemens Automation in establishing a Metrics Program by introduction within a pilot or show-case project organization. The organization in which the pilot Metrics Program was applied is located in Erlangen, Germany. The types of products that are developed are automation systems for machine tools and robots. The software development activities can be described as the development of embedded real-time systems. The software is typically written in C and Assembler on PC-based workstations, and then embedded as PROM-based software within microprocessor-controlled products.

This organization initiated the use of metrics using the Seven-Step Metrics Introduction Program approach described in Chapter 4. After application to the pilot project organization (for approximately six months), the Metrics Program will be revised based upon the pilot experience, and then introduced and sold throughout this organization. This section does not contain significant experience gathered over years. It does, however, provide some additional practical examples of basic and global metrics.

9.6.2 Measured Values

This Siemens Automation organization has defined twelve measured values that correspond to their quality improvement goals and their software development process. These measured values are all counts of faults, time, size, and costs, and thus are not *calculated* metrics. The measured values are the 'sensors' of the product development process, and they are used to calculate the *basic* or *global* metrics. The definition of the measured values, the methods to collect them, and the responsible organizations, are defined for the pilot project organization. The Siemens Automation pilot project measured values are given below.

- **M1** = The number of faults found during Functional Test for each software version.

- **M2** = The number of faults found during Acceptance Test for each software version.

- **M3** = The development cost of a software version measured from the beginning of the project to the actual product release measured in Staff-Months.

- **M4** = The planned and actual product release dates.

- **M5** = The project duration in months measured from the beginning of the project to the actual product release date.

- **M6** = The number of lines of code added or modified for the current release as compared to the previous release. This is measured as delta lines of code or KDLOC as defined by the Siemens standard and measured with the PROLOC tool.

- **M7** = The number of net lines of code (KNLOC) for the product software version. This is also provided by the PROLOC tool. It is defined as delivered source lines of code not counting comments and blank lines.

The measured values given above are derived from the product development process for each software version release. The measured values given below apply to products that have been released and are being used by customers in the field. Thus these measured values apply to the maintenance process, and they are reported on a product model basis which may have multiple software versions in the field.

- **M8** = The number of field faults found per week. These values are also counted or averaged over a quarter for longer term trend analysis depending on the time window of interest.

- **M9** = The number of customer change requests per week. These values are also counted or averaged over a quarter for longer term trend analysis depending on the time window of interest.

- **M10** = The number of open field faults found but not yet corrected.

- **M11** = The number of open customer change requests identified but not yet resolved.

- **M12** = The maintenance cost per quarter reported in Staff-Months.

9.6.3 Basic Metrics

Siemens Automation has defined fifteen *basic* metrics. These metrics are *calculated* metrics using the measured values given above. These *global* metrics are used for managing, decision-making, and providing development process improvement insights and feedback. The basic metrics are broken down into classes of metrics corresponding to the characteristics and responsibilities of the development process areas of improvement. The metric labeling scheme corresponds to these improvement areas of interest. Four areas of improvement have been identified.

- **Product Quality (Q).** These metrics measure aspects of the product quality in terms of the number of faults found during the various product development process phases.

- **Change Requests (Ä).** These metrics measure the change requests received from customers. Change requests are separated from fault reports (Q) found in the field. Change requests reflect the customers' desire to have different features and functionality in the product than that provided.

These metrics measure the effectiveness of the organization to specify and develop products that are useful to the customers.

- **Productivity (P).** These metrics measure the effectiveness of the development and maintenance process.

- **Schedule (T).** These metrics measure the ability of the development organization for adhering to their planned schedules.

The Product Quality metrics are defined below.

- **Q1** = The number of functional test faults (M1) divided by the delta lines of code (M6). This metric is calculated from data collected during Functional Test.

- **Q2** = The number of acceptance test faults (M2) divided by the delta lines of code (M6). This metric is calculated from data collected during the Acceptance Test phase.

- **Q3** = The number of field faults found per week (M8).

- **Q4** = The field faults per week (M8) divided by the net lines of code (M7).

- **Q5** = The field faults per week (M8) divided by the delta lines of code (M6). Metrics Q4 and Q5 provide an indication of the maturity level and reliability of the released product.

- **Q6** = The number of open field faults found but not yet corrected (M10).

- **Q7** = The number of open field faults (M10) divided by the net lines of code (M7). Metrics Q6 and Q7 provide an indication of the maintenance process concerning fault correction.

The Change Requests metrics are defined below.

- **Ä1** = The number of customer change requests per week (M9).

- **Ä2** = The number of customer change requests per week (M9) divided by the net lines of code (M7).

- **Ä3** = The number of open customer change requests (M11).

- **Ä4** = The number of open customer change requests (M11) divided by the net lines of code (M7).

The Productivity metrics are defined below.

- **P1** = The delta lines of code (M6) divided by the development cost (M3).

- **P2** = The maintenance cost (M12) divided by 100 times the net lines of code (M7).

The Schedule metrics are defined below.

- **T1** = The difference between the actual software release date (M4) and the desired (planned) release date (M4) in work-days.

- **T2** = The schedule deviation (T1) in months divided by the project duration (M5) times 100%.

9.6.4 Metrics Summary

This Siemens Automation organization has implemented a pilot project for Metrics Program introduction. They have defined a number of basic metrics consistent with their software development process and quality improvement goals. They have applied the Seven-Step Metrics Introduction Program approach.

This Siemens Automation organization has defined twelve measured values as summarized in Table 9.1. The units used and the organization responsible for generating the metrics are indicated.

Siemens Automation has also defined fifteen basic metrics. These metrics are calculated from the measured values. The basic metrics, their units, and their improvement areas are summarized in Table 9.2. The relationships of the basic metrics to the software development process are summarized in Figure 9.14.

The metrics will be further refined based upon the experience of the pilot project. In addition, significant effort will be applied to defining the methods for metric feedback reporting, and defining and coordinating the activities for development process improvement.

Table 9.1 Measured Values

Metric	*Units*	*Organization*
M1 - Functional Test Faults	Faults	Development
M2 - Acceptance Test Faults	Faults	System Test
M3 - Development Cost	Staff-Months	Finance
M4 - Release Dates	Dates	System Test
M5 - Project Duration	Months	Product Planning
M6 - Delta LOC	KDLOC	Development
M7 - Net LOC	KNLOC	Development
M8 - Field Faults	Faults/Week	System Test
M9 - Customer Change Requests	Change Requests/Week	System Test
M10 - Open Field Faults	Faults	System Test
M11 - Open Customer Change Requests	Change Requests	System Test
M12 - Maintenance Cost	Staff-Months/Quarter	Finance

Table 9.2 Basic Metrics

Metric	*Units*	*Improvement Area*
Q1 - Functional Test Effectiveness	Faults/KDLOC	Product Quality
Q2 - Acceptance Test Effectiveness	Faults/KDLOC	Product Quality
Q3 - Field Faults	Faults/Week	Product Quality
Q4 - Normalized Field Faults (Net)	Faults/Week/ KNLOC	Product Quality
Q5 - Normalized Field Faults (Delta)	Faults/Week/ KDLOC	Product Quality
Q6 - Open Field Faults	Faults	Product Quality
Q7 - Normalized Open Field Faults (Net)	Faults/KNLOC	Product Quality
Ä1 - Customer Change Requests	Change Requests/Week	Product Quality
Ä2 - Normalized Customer Change Requests	Requests/Week/ KNLOC	Product Quality
Ä3 - Open Customer Change Requests	Change Requests	Product Quality
Ä4 - Normalized Open Customer Change Requests	Requests/KNLOC	Product Quality
P1 - Development Productivity	DLOC/Staff-Month	Productivity
P2 - Maintenance Productivity	Staff-Months /Qtr./KNLOC	Productivity

T1 - Schedule Deviation	Work Days	Schedule
T2 - Relative Schedule Deviation	%	Schedule

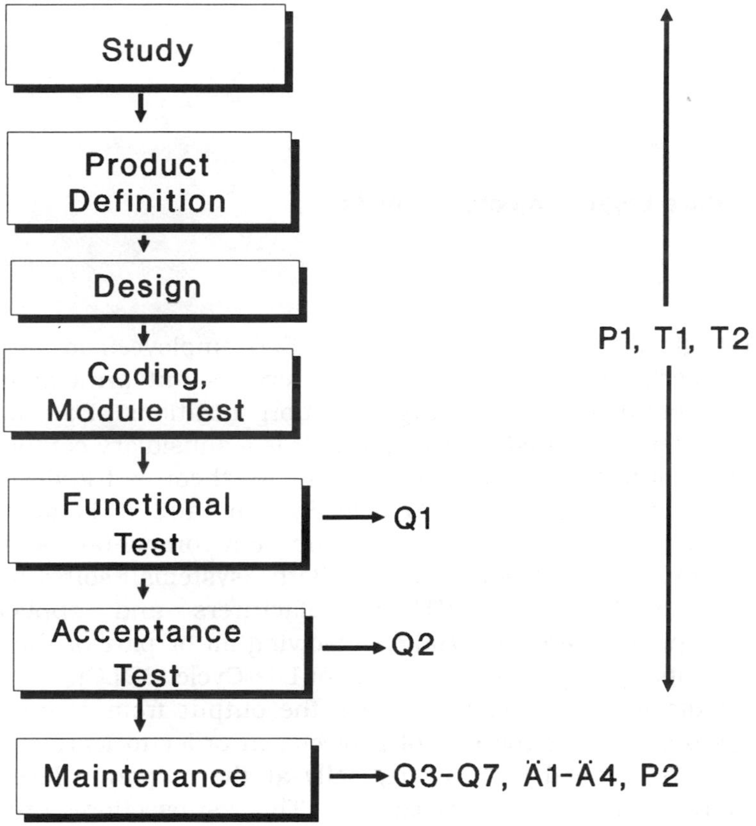

Figure 9.14 Basic Metrics Related to the Software Development Process.

10 Best Practices and Benefits Experience - Data Logic

10.1 Data Logic Projects Analysis

10.1.1 Projects Overview

Data Logic Limited is a company of 500 employees founded in 1967, offering a variety of computer services but principally the development of software for large client organizations. Data Logic's headquarters is located near London. It is a subsidiary company of Raytheon of Lexington, Massachusetts. Raytheon is the developer of the Patriot Air Defense Missile System, and it is active in electronics, aviation, industrial and environmental services, publishing, and construction. Both systems software for Information Technology (IT) manufacturers and application software projects are undertaken involving all or part of the Data Logic company's Systems Development Life-Cycle (SDLC).

Periodically, Data Logic analyses the output from termination reports produced at the end of projects, in order to learn lessons that can be applied both strategically at the corporate level and tactically within new projects. This subsection presents information from the latest of such analyses, issued in January 1991, covering projects completed in the preceding eighteen months. It provides examples of how global metrics are used for project management.

A total of nineteen projects were analyzed, ranging in effort from a 93 staff-day consultancy study to a 36 staff-year coding and testing development. The average effort was approximately five staff-years.

10.1.2 Development Process

The Data Logic product development process is called the Systems Development Life-Cycle (SDLC). The SDLC contains the following development phases:

FRS	Functional Requirement Specification
FS	Functional Specification
DS	Design Specification (including Program Specification)
CUT	Code & Unit Test
ST	Systems Testing
IMP	Implementation.

The Implementation Phase includes the preparation for live operation; e.g. Training, User Documentation, and Client Support during Acceptance Testing. Clients normally purchase a maintenance contract if they require Data Logic's involvement during live operation.

Many clients develop the Functional Requirement Specification themselves; i.e., they approach Data Logic after the need for the system has been justified. Many also have predefined functionality requirements. Taking these variations of starting point into consideration, this analysis divides the projects into four groups:

A	Full SDLC (4 projects)
B	Design, Code, Test, and Implement (6 projects)
C	Code, Test, and Implement (4 projects)
D	Non-Standard (Porting, Studies, etc. - 5 projects).

Group C includes projects which used the Data Logic Application Development Center (ADC), where programs are developed with the Micro Focus Workbench tools on PCs before the tested code is migrated to the client's mainframe.

10.1.3 Metrics Used

The Project Termination Report is completed by the Project Manager, who early in the project cycle will have agreed with the Quality Management (QM) Department as to the metrics which are to be collected. For simple projects the metrics collected are those defined by the Company's Project Control System (PCS), and they are documented within the Quality Plan for the project. The metrics include:

- Staff-days of effort originally planned for completion of the project, by phase;

- Staff-days of effort estimated during the progression of the project for implementing agreed changes to functionality (System Variation Requests or SVRs);

- Actual staff-days of effort expended against the original plan, by phase;

- Actual staff-days of effort spent implementing SVRs.

These metrics allow for checking of the accuracy of estimating, both by phase and for the project in total. Performance against the planned duration and the time growth of the project can be measured. The addition of financial rates, of course, allows for the monitoring of the sales margin.

For more complex projects the metrics requirements are more detailed and they are documented in a Metrics Plan, which is cross-referenced from the Quality Plan. In this analysis, full Metrics Plans were used in four of the six most recent projects.

The additional required metrics varied, but in all cases included:

- Sizing metrics (KLOC), defined as thousands of lines of uncommented procedural code measured at the point of handover from unit testing to systems testing;

- The number of Software Difficulty Reports (SDRs - potential errors/defects) identified, resolved, and outstanding at weekly intervals throughout the Systems Testing and

Implementation Phases;

- The level of criticality of Software Difficulty Reports (critical, serious, minor, cosmetic);

- The number of programs, modules.

In some projects, Function Point counts were also taken. For the period covered, however, there was no company policy requiring the use of this technique (Albrecht, 1979).

10.1.4 Quality Improvement Techniques

The projects under review used a variety of quality improvement techniques, individually specified in the Quality Plan for the project. Data Logic's policy is that work is bid assuming the use of a known set of standards, methodologies, and tools; be they proprietary, Data Logic's own, the client's own, or a mixture of all three.

If a client requires that specific additional quality techniques be applied, these will be implemented at the client's cost. Thus, while the use of inspections and walkthroughs are part of the company standards, the level and quantity of such review processes will vary from project to project. For example, only two of the projects within the last analysis required the use of a Defect Removal Model. The use of such a Defect Removal Model on a project enables the project manager to predict the number of errors likely to be introduced and removed at various phases of the SDLC.

All Group A, B, and C projects used code inspections, and all but two Group A and B projects used a 'Fagan style' inspection of their design specifications (Fagan, 1976). In the remaining cases, the design was walked through with the client against the Functional Specification document. By the nature of their work, Group D projects were not reviewed using the above techniques.

Data Logic is well aware that both product quality and software productivity greatly depend on the development process. Therefore Data Logic regularly assesses the quality of the software development and management process for all major projects.

These evaluations cover the effective use of:

- Management methods and practices, plus their documentation

- Tools and automated processes
- Training of staff
- Operational and technical interfaces
- Technical standards.

The evaluations are carried out by an independent qualified auditor against predefined checklists, using a modified version of the SEI (Software Engineering Institute, Pittsburgh, USA) assessment method (Humphrey, 1987). Management receives the audit report and takes appropriate action on any deficiencies.

These assessments have proved particularly useful in the areas of:

- Project initiation and planning
- Investment decisions
- Quality planning and productivity programs.

10.1.5 Benefits

The benefits from the use of software metrics can only be put into perspective if the cost of the entire quality program is quantified and controlled. Once a commitment is made to the production of quality products through quality processes, the cost and benefits of the quality process must be measured in order to identify changes in the overall level of quality.

A common difficulty with quality improvement programs is that normally it is a company's senior management that makes the decision to improve quality as a long-term goal. The program itself however, will involve additional work for some individuals who may not be able to identify any short-term benefits to themselves.

Data Logic has an advantage in that the requirement for production of a Metrics Plan was upgraded from an advisory to a mandatory requirement when Data Logic was undertaking full project responsibility. As such, project managers included an allowance in their original plans for the metrics activity. Team members were then encouraged to see the work content as part of their personal contribution to the overall quality improvement program.

Some individual staff comments are reproduced below:

> - 'Since most of the process was automated, I found it took very little extra effort. I did not make use of the output myself, that went to the Systems Test Managers.' (by a programmer)
>
> - 'I assumed the information had been requested by the client and we were being paid to provide it.' (by a programmer)
>
> - 'The metrics on the rate of clearing SDRs helped me convince the client of the need for more resources.' (by a project manager)

The most negative reactions came from those staff who were required to collect metrics data without a corresponding increase in their work schedule. This was a problem when the project manager underestimated the effort involved when preparing his original Project Plan.

Client reaction on the whole was favorable. They saw the use to which the project managers put the metrics as proof of the added value of using a more quality conscious software supplier. In particular, they appreciated the early warning and subsequent planning for or avoidance of potential problems with budgets and schedules.

The benefits of assessing the quality and software productivity process are seen in the quantitative statements which can be made about the company and projects' strengths and weaknesses. The modified SEI questionnaire proved to be of great value in creating 'exception lists' for management action. At the company level, Data Logic devised a method of summarizing the results from a range of projects and effectively prioritizing the areas which required action. On the other hand, the overall assessed process maturity level rating of the company had little obvious business application.

However, at the project level the maturity level rating was seen as beneficial in confirming the level of quality in the processes being used. The prioritized list of questions which were answered 'NO', also helped to identify areas where a project could improve the process.

It was necessary to create a tool to handle the questionnaire answers and to present the results. Initially a spreadsheet was used but it had limitations. A development is currently under way to introduce a more powerful tool with more extensive analysis and presentation capabilities.

10.2 Data Logic Billing System

10.2.1 Application Overview

The application described in this subsection is a Miscellaneous Billing System implemented across Europe for a multi-national automotive company. The System produces billing documents which:

- Require a customer to pay (an invoice or a debit note adjusting a previously raised invoice)

- Advise a customer that his account has been credited (normally a credit note adjusting a previously raised invoice or a 'self-billing invoice')

- Facilitate customer importing of material through customs.

Much of the data which appears on the Miscellaneous Billing Documents is transferred to associated computer systems such as Receivables and General Ledger.

The objectives of the System were as follows:

- To replace the existing manual and automated procedures with an IBM mainframe system providing:

  Single Billings
  Summary Billings
  Formalized approach to billing structure and content
  Automatic account number validation
  Assisted revenue analysis with mandatory balancing
  Predefined default values to reduce keystrokes
  Laser printing of billing documents

On-line progression of billings through to existing receivables and revenue systems
On-line display of billings
Text library facilities
Archive and copy invoice facilities

- To provide functionality which has taken European requirements into account

- To provide a consistent document numbering system for all Miscellaneous Billing Documents

- To provide interfaces to Receivables, General Ledger, and other systems

- To assist in the revision of Sales Accounting office practices.

10.2.2 Development Process

10.2.2.1 Overview

This development was a Data Logic fixed-price managed project made up of the coding and unit testing of COBOL programs, a system test, and support throughout the client's acceptance test. The baseline for the development was a complete set of program specifications, prepared by Data Logic as part of an earlier contract, which had been signed off by the client's systems and user representatives. Most of the work was performed on the client's site using its IBM mainframe development facilities (ISPF/TSO, COBOL, CICS, DB2). However, a small programming team additionally developed some of the programs with Data Logic's own PC-based development center using MicroFocus Workbench tools. The peak team size was seventeen, made up of the project manager, a technical/database specialist, three team leaders, and twelve programmers.

10.2.2.2 Management and Reporting

The project manager was ultimately responsible for the successful and timely completion of the contracted deliverables, and for reporting progress to both the client and Data Logic sector management. Formal documented meetings were held as follows:

- Weekly progress meetings between the Data Logic project manager and the client's systems and user representatives.

- Monthly steering meetings were held with the client to review progress, issues, and concerns related to all aspects of the delivery of the system. This included tasks relating to acceptance testing, user documentation, and training, all of which were the client's responsibility.

- Monthly tracking meetings were held internally by Data Logic, chaired by an independent tracking manager, to review progress and discuss any risks and exposures.

The project manager monitored and controlled the development using Data Logic's Project Control System (PCS), which was supplemented in the planning phase by the use of the Project Manager Workbench (PMW).

10.2.2.3 Project Structure, Plans, and Standards

The project manager had four staff members directly reporting to him:

- Three team leaders each responsible for a team of four programmers, and for a limited amount of personal programming work.

- One senior technician with responsibility for

    . providing data base and technical support to the rest of the team

    . writing the system test strategy and plans

    . managing and performing the system test.

The project team worked within the constraints of the following project specific standards in addition to the company standards and procedures (e.g. PCS, Inspection Techniques, System Test Plan).

10.2.2.3.1 Quality Plan

The Quality Plan is a definition of the methods used by Data Logic in undertaking the project and the quality standards observed. It identified:

- The key players in the management of the project (on both sides).
- The method of reporting and the schedule of formal meetings.
- The schedule of tasks to be undertaken by the client and Data Logic to enable the contractual obligations to be satisfied.
- The development environment.
- A summary of the configuration control procedures to be used on the project to manage change.
- A summary of the quality reviews and inspections to be undertaken by the Data Logic development team.

10.2.2.3.2 Configuration Control Plan

The Configuration Control Plan included details of the configuration control procedures that were used by the Data Logic team with regard to the creation of and changes to:

- The baseline documentation;
- Other contracted deliverables (program folders, system test plan);
- Standards specific to the project.

10.2.2.3.3 Metrics Plan

The metrics plan is a description of the metrics which would be collected and analyzed in order to:

- Provide information on productivity;
- Assist in the prediction of completion dates;
- Highlight possible problem areas to facilitate possible corrective actions;
- Provide feedback on the effectiveness of corrective actions;
- Indicate the level of quality;
- Provide statistics for inclusion in the company model.

10.2.2.3.4 Client's Programming and DB2 Standards

Specific coding standards were established by the client for this project, which was their first DB2 project.

10.2.2.3.5 Program Development Standard

The Program Development Standard contains the methods and procedures followed by the programming team for the development and documentation of the programs. It details the actions that the programmer must undertake in order to produce a completed deliverable which fulfils the contracted requirements, and is acceptable to the client.

10.2.3 Metrics Used

Data Logic's PCS was used to plan the hierarchy of activities and tasks, allocate responsibilities, identify planned budgets and schedules for each task, and record actual effort taken on each task. In addition, the following metrics were captured for each of the 112 programs developed:

- Actual lines of code (LOC), excluding labels,

comments, and blank lines; the total for this project was 103 KLOC.

- The number of System Difficulty Reports (SDRs) counted during both system testing and acceptance testing.

The plans and metrics were used as described below.

10.2.3.1 Earned Value Analysis

The planned schedule budgets were based on an average estimate depending on the complexity of the program (simple, small, medium, complex, very complex).

A schedule of achievement was produced by the project manager based on the value of low-level tasks and their planned completion dates. As tasks were completed, this achievement value was measured against the schedule to give an indication of the overall slippage against the original time-scales. In practice it was not easy to use this variance to quantify the level of corrective action to take, but it certainly highlighted the need. The planning tool was used to examine the impact of additional resources on the schedule time-scales.

10.2.3.2 Ratio of LOC per Staff-Day for each Program

These metrics enabled the project manager to assess and predict an average expectation for the productivity of the team members, and a comparison to the productivity of other recent Data Logic projects in similar environments.

After the initial learning curve which most of the team experienced, an acceptable productivity rate was achieved by the team. The experienced programmers achieved a level of productivity approximately 30% higher than the junior members of the team. This compared very favorably to two other concurrent projects and against general expectations. However, it was recognized that the team was working extended hours which, when taken into account, reduced the productivity by 33% to a level which was still considered acceptable. It was observed that the inexperienced staff members generally reached acceptable productivity levels after two programs.

The fact that the project was slipping against the original

planned schedule time-scales despite the acceptable productivity rates indicated that the estimates had been understated. This was attributed to many of the programs being more complex than was initially envisioned.

10.2.3.3 Lines of Code

The size of programs still to be developed or completed was estimated based on any similarity with programs which had already been completed. This sizing, and therefore the related number of required staff-days of effort, proved to be unreliable. Subsequently, re-estimation of the remaining programs was based on a revised average number of staff-days for each level of complexity.

10.2.3.4 SDRs Counted per Program

The number of SDRs counted per program in the system and acceptance test phase, as compared to that expected by Data Logic, along with the amount of effort required to fix the SDRs, were used to:

- Measure the quality of the delivered programs;
- Provide a basis on which to estimate the remaining effort required to complete the testing.

10.2.4 Quality Improvement Techniques

10.2.4.1 Mid-Project

All standards and contracted deliverables were subject to formal walkthroughs and inspections. The Quality Plan and other project specific standards, written by the Data Logic project manager, were submitted to Data Logic's Quality Management (QM) Department for approval and authorization.

During the programming phase, walkthroughs were performed by the team leaders on completion of the program design, the unit test plan, the first cleanly compiled source program, and the final program folder containing the test results. All walkthroughs were formally documented, and the number of defects at each stage recorded.

The System Test Strategy was reviewed and approved by both the project manager and QM, and the System Test Plan was inspected and approved by the project manager.

An internal audit was performed by Data Logic's QM at which ten deficiencies were recorded, seven minor and three warnings. These were followed up by the project manager resulting in corrective action being taken to remedy five of the minor discrepancies. On review it was agreed with QM that no further action needed to be taken on the other five items.

10.2.4.2 Post-Project

Following completion of the project, a termination report was completed by the project manager which recorded management and technical problems encountered on the project and summarized all of the metrics collected during the development. The metrics were identified where programs were subject to the initial learning curve, and also where commonality would have reduced the effort taken.

The management and technical problems were reviewed by QM and a technical director, and discussed with the project manager. The metrics were analyzed by the technical director. The following are a selection of the deductions made:

- Complexity ratings are not in themselves an adequate predictor of effort. There was no significant difference in the effort required to complete programs ranging from simple to medium complexity.

- There was no strong correlation between complexity ratings and productivity rates (LOC/day).

- Coding rate is not an adequate predictor of effort at the individual program level. Hence, there would appear to be little advantage in attempting to predict the size of programs as a method of estimation.

- There was a strong correlation between complexity and program size.

- There was a concern over the number of very large programs (14%).

The QM Department carried out an SEI assessment to establish the effectiveness of the following on the project:

- Use of methods
- Use of tools and automated processes/controls
- Use of defined management procedures and policies
- Level of staff skill and their training
- Use of technical standards
- Effectiveness of operational and technical interfaces.

The project achieved the SEI maturity level 2 demonstrating that it had standardized methods facilitating repeatable processes. The specific weaknesses identified were subsequently compared to output from assessments of other projects in order to establish any commonality.

10.2.5 Benefits

The main advantages which were gained from the collection and analysis of the metrics are summarized below.

10.2.5.1 Quantitative Measurement of Development Team Productivity

The project manager had an objective measure of development team productivity which was measured in LOC per staff-day while taking into account reused code. This measure highlighted the problem of the difficulty of estimation for predicting code sizes and anticipated productivity.

10.2.5.2 Quantitative Measurement of Quality

By recording the number of SDRs discovered in each program, it was possible to identify poor quality in the unit testing. Testing techniques were examined and corrective actions were taken.

10.2.5.3 Basis for Re-Estimation

By having a set of metrics which could be used to identify changing trends on the project (e.g. the effort needed to develop a program of a particular size or complexity rating), different options became more visible to the project manager for re-estimating the total effort for project completion.

10.2.5.4 Tracking and Reporting

The availability of metrics to provide visual summaries of progress and performance assisted senior management in their understanding of the reports produced for tracking, steering, and progress meetings.

10.2.5.5 Comparison Against Other Projects

Metrics collected on this project were analyzed by Data Logic's QM, and compared with those collected from other projects across the company. This analysis was used to provide recommendations and trends for estimators and planners of future work.

10.3 Data Logic Networked PC Environment Products

This section contains information relating to a number of projects carried out by Data Logic for large computer manufacturers within the past five years. Generally the purpose of the projects was to develop products for networked PC environments. The metrics described provide examples of the application of global metrics.

The client companies were experienced product developers with many existing standards and procedures which Data Logic was required to follow. Where they had no defined standard, for example for the C coding language, Data Logic standards were used or new standards were developed. The client companies were also very familiar with metrics, and required their use in the planning stage and throughout the developments.

10.3.1 Development Process

10.3.1.1 Environment

The development environment for all these projects was UNIX-based. The reason for using UNIX rather than other PC operating systems such as DOS was the proliferation of tools which existed for the UNIX platform, and the familiarity that the development teams had with those tools. Of particular importance were configuration control tools, product-build facilities, shared access and shared processing power.

10.3.1.2 Software Process

The software development process used for all projects was very similar to the Data Logic Software Development Life-Cycle (SDLC). This process is described in the following sections. It was almost identical for all the developments with the exception of some degree of overlapping of the test stages.

10.3.1.2.1 Specification of Requirements

For these projects the customers had responsibility for the specification of the requirements although on some of the projects input was provided by the senior Data Logic technical staff.

10.3.1.2.2 Start-Up Stage

During this stage a number of project initiation documents were produced. These included the Quality Plan, the Project Plan, and the Metrics Plan. The Quality Plan defined the deliverables, quality processes, standards and acceptance criteria for the project; the Project Plan defined the procedures, resources and the schedule for the project; the Metrics Plan defined which statistics would be collected, how that collection would be achieved and the purposes for which they would be used.

This stage was overlapped with the Functional Specification and High-Level Design stage in order that reasonably accurate estimates for product size and complexity were available for use in the preparation of the Project Plan.

10.3.1.2.3 Functional Specification and High-Level Design Stage

During this stage the Functional Specification and High-Level Design or System Architecture documents were produced by the System Architect with support from the senior designers on the team. As the names imply, these documents defined the functionality and the architecture of the product to be developed. The architectural definition included a breakdown of the product into a number of components.

Additional deliverables from this stage included a Build Plan, which is not a standard Data Logic deliverable, and the strategy documents for the Integration and System Test stages.

The Build Plan defined the means by which the components of the product were to be integrated, the sequence in which this would occur, the hardware and software requirements to achieve that, and the output of the build process in terms of partial or complete systems. For these projects the system was composed of a number of C source files which were compiled and linked into libraries and into executable programs; the process was controlled by the UNIX 'make' utility which ensures that the compilations and links occur in the required order. The standard UNIX Source Code Control System, SCCS, was used to ensure that the correct version of each source file was used for each build. The output from the build process consisted of either partial or complete systems. Partial systems could consist of anything from one or two source files which were interdependent and could reasonably be tested as a unit, to almost complete systems which could be used to test large areas of functionality. Each build was defined in terms of the source files or components of which it was composed and the areas of functionality which it provided.

The test strategy documents defined which aspects of the product would be tested at each stage together with the test coverage and type of testing that would be used to achieve it. They also outlined the hardware and software needs of the test stages.

10.3.1.2.4 Design, Code, and Unit Test Stage

Most of the deliverables for this stage were the responsibility of the Development Team. These included the Low-Level Design documents and the product code. The design documents consisted of one design document for each component outlining the functionality and architecture of the component, and a design document for each module within the components describing the interface and detailed design for that module. The Unit Test Plans relevant to each unit were included in each document.

The development of the Information Units also took place during this stage. These include the hard-copy documentation such as user and programmer reference material and on-line Information Units such as contextual help and on-line reference material.

While these development activities were in progress the Integration and System Test Teams prepared their detailed Test Plans, the code for the manual tests, and the scripts for the automated tests.

10.3.1.2.5 Integration Test Stage

The purpose of this stage was to combine the modules and components which make up the product and to ensure that they interact as specified in the High- and Low-Level Design documents. It included the tasks of building test builds, as defined in the Build Strategy, testing those builds according to the Integration Test Plan using the manual and automated tests, and the correction of defects which those tests detected. The process was repeated using increasingly higher functionality builds until a build of the complete product had been tested and had reached the quality level defined in the Quality Plan.

It was always intended that this stage should not start until the Design, Code, and Unit Test stage was complete. In practice this was not practical and Integration Testing generally started while the code and unit test of some modules was still in progress. The integration of those modules took place later in this stage.

10.3.1.2.6 System Test Stage

The purpose of this stage was to test that the product as developed provided the functionality which was defined in the Functional Specification and any subsequent approved change requests. The product was tested according to the System Test Plan using the test scripts and test programs which were developed for that purpose. The defects which those tests detected were corrected and the tests re-run.

This stage was deemed to be complete when the acceptance criteria for the Acceptance Test Stage, as defined in the Quality Plan, were achieved. Again it was not intended that this stage should overlap with the Integration Test stage. However, it proved useful to release incomplete builds to the System Test Team to allow them to test their processes and test programs.

10.3.1.2.7 Acceptance Test Stage

This stage was the responsibility of the customers' own Test Teams. They prepared and executed the tests and a Data Logic support team corrected any defects which those tests detected.

10.3.1.3 Standards

In all the projects the standards were a combination of customer standards, Data Logic standards and project specific standards. All the standards were identified in the Quality Plan at the start of the projects.

In general the higher-level documents, such as the Functional Specification, High-Level Design, Test Strategies and Plans, were covered by customer standards. The low-level design documentation required the definition of project specific standards, and the Data Logic code and test standards were used with some amendment to address specific customer requirements.

10.3.1.4 Methodologies

A specific design method was not used on any of these projects. A topdown approach combined with some aspects of object-oriented design was used. This approach proved satisfactory and more formal methods such as Yourdon or Z were not considered necessary.

10.3.1.5 Project Team Structure

The project team size differed on each project in proportion to the size of the product under development but the structure, as illustrated in Figure 10.1, remained fundamentally the same.

The Development Teams were responsible for the production of the Low-Level Design Documents, for coding the system, for producing and executing the unit tests, and for correcting defects found by that process. Some of that team then went on to fix any faults detected during the Integration, System, and Acceptance Test stages.

The Information Development Teams were responsible for the production of the on-line and hard-copy Information Units.

The Integration Test and System Test Teams were responsible for the planning, preparation, and execution of the tests for their respective test stages.

The Quality Teams were responsible for the definition of the standards for the projects, for monitoring adherence to those standards, for the moderation of all document inspections, for the inspection of code, and for the collection and analysis of metrics.

Due to the size and complexity of the development and test environments, an Environment Support Team was necessary to ensure that the project teams had the constant access to the tools which they needed. This support team was responsible for developing and acquiring tools, for establishing the appropriate hardware and software environments, and for ensuring its availability at all times.

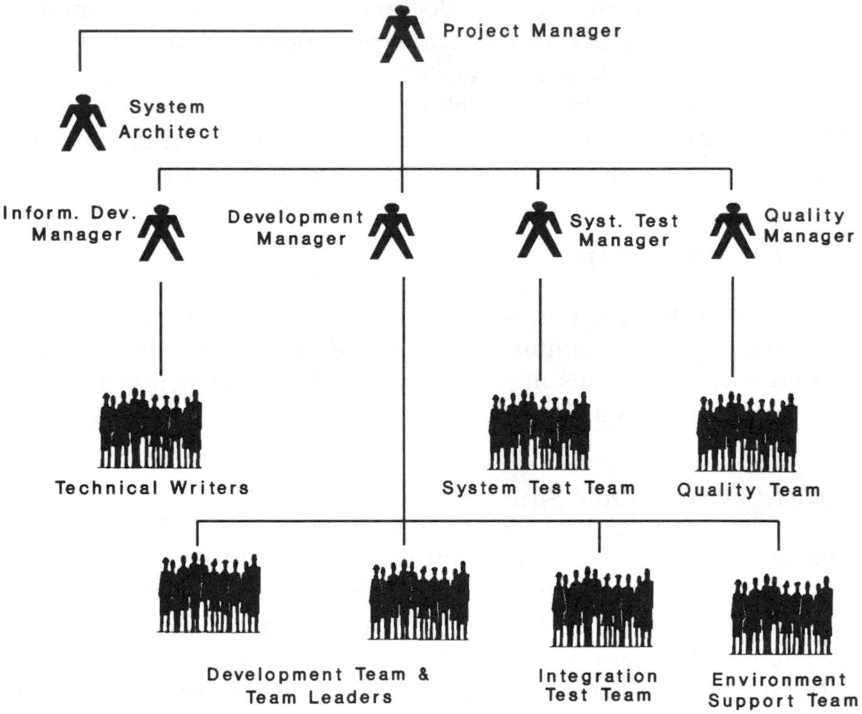

Figure 10.1 Team Structure.

10.3.2 Metrics Used

Metrics were used as a management tool on all these projects. A number of statistics relating to the size, productivity, and quality of the product were collected throughout the project.

10.3.2.1 Sizing Metrics

Product size was measured in Lines of Code (LOC). The difficulty with this means of measurement is arriving at a satisfactory definition of what a line of code is. For these projects it was deemed to be a line of executable product code. All trace statements, test programs, comments, and blank lines were excluded.

The size of the product was initially estimated during production of the Functional Specification. As details of the architecture and internal workings of the modules became clear these initial estimates are reviewed and refined. An LOC counting tool was written which counted the valid lines in completed code to give actual figures to compare against those estimates.

Estimates were also made of the number of test cases required during Integration and System Testing and actual numbers were manually monitored.

10.3.2.2 Productivity Metrics

Statistics regarding productivity were collected in the following areas:

- code and unit test rate, measured in average LOC per staff-day;
- test case preparation rate, measured in average test case per staff-day;
- test case execution rate, measured in average test cases per staff-day for first run and for subsequent runs;
- defect correction rate, measured in average defects fixed per staff-day.

Information regarding the effort required for these tasks was acquired from the project control system, so detailed task breakdown was essential.

10.3.2.3 Quality Metrics

At the customers' request Defect Removal Models (DRMs) were defined at the start of each project. Quality statistics were then collected in terms of defects detected per KLOC at all stages of the development cycle.

During the Functional Specification and Design stages the necessary information was easily obtained as the defects detected during the inspection process were logged in the appropriate reports.

During the code and unit test stage it was extremely difficult to count the number of defects. The person responsible for coding a module was also responsible for unit testing it. This led to a number of operational problems such as deciding when the coding task was complete and the unit test stage had started, and how to easily log the defects. Counting the defects from this stage was not a success.

During the later, more formal test stages all defects were recorded in the Data Logic System Difficulty Reporting (SDR) system. As this system was also used to record information regarding the validity of the defects, the required information was easy to obtain. This actual data could then be compared with the Defect Removal Model allowing early detection of deviations from plan.

10.3.3 Quality Improvement Techniques

A number of quality improvement techniques were used on all these projects and are described below.

10.3.3.1 Standards

The Quality Team defined standards for all documents, for the product code and for the testing process early in the development life-cycle. Clear standards helped the Development Team to produce documents and code more quickly and more completely. Consistency of layout resulted in easier-to-use documentation and code that was easier to maintain and enhance.

10.3.3.2 Quality Targets

The Quality Team also defined the quality targets for each deliverable, for each stage of the development life-cycle. Actual quality was compared with these targets, allowing early identification of quality problems and early corrective action.

10.3.3.3 Design Walkthroughs

The designer of the more complex components of the systems held design walkthroughs with the System Architect and other designers to clarify the requirements for the component, to explain its interface, and to allow early opportunities to identify design problems.

10.3.3.4 Formal Inspections and Informal Reviews

Most documents and a sample of the code were formally inspected by both client and Data Logic personnel. Although these projects preceded the existence of the Data Logic standard for inspections, the processes, based on Fagan techniques (Fagan, 1976), are very similar. Other documents and code were informally reviewed. The selection of code samples ensured that some code from every component was inspected with the emphasis on inspecting the areas which had most defects at the design stage. The review process identified and logged defects, but did not include the formal meeting.

These processes provided an opportunity for the identification and agreement of defects. The process also allowed the Quality Team to count defects at each stage and to compare actual data with the quality targets.

10.3.3.5 Testing

Test procedures, designed to identify as many defects as possible, were used at every stage. These procedures included the following:

> preparation of an overall test strategy which identified what attributes of the product should be tested, the test phase responsible for that testing, how they should be tested, and the hardware and software needs of the test teams;

- preparation of an Integration Test Strategy and Plan which were based on the Build Plan and identified the sequence of integration and testing of the system and the tests which must be prepared and executed; integration test preparation and execution was the responsibility of a separate Integration Test Team which worked closely with the software Development Team;

- preparation of a System Test Strategy and Plan which identified the aspects of the system that would be tested and the tests which must be prepared and executed;

- regression testing of changed code.

10.3.3.6 Change Request Procedure

Careful management of change is an important factor in producing a quality product. Change requests often result in rework to completed design documents and code; this rework is unlikely to be subjected to the same rigorous inspection and test procedure as the original work. The Data Logic System Variation Request (SVR) process ensured that the impact of every change request was properly assessed and that the effort to do the necessary re-review, re-inspection and regression testing was factored into the cost of the change. The decision to implement the change or defer it was then based on this information.

10.3.3.7 Configuration Control

Configuration control procedures, based on the UNIX Source Code Control System (SCCS), were used throughout the development life-cycle for the following purposes:

- to ensure that everyone had access to the most up-to-date documents and code while being prevented from accessing work in progress which is frequently inconsistent and untested;

- to ensure that each version of the system can be recovered should changes prove unnecessary or problematic;

- to ensure that each released version of the system can be re-created in the event of problems with the release media or a need to rerun previous versions.

10.3.4 Benefits Gained

It was very difficult to quantify the benefits of using metrics. On these projects we did not have to convince the customers of the benefits, as it was they who required that we collect and use the statistics and follow the quality processes.

All the metrics statistics were used for two purposes; i.e., to compare actual progress and quality against plan during the development, and as the basis for planning later projects. As a guide to how the project was proceeding against plan, the use of metrics was less useful on the first of these projects than on the later ones. This was partly due to the inexperience of the team in the accumulation and use of such statistics, and also because the initial estimates for productivity, product size, and quality were based on only a small amount of statistical data from previous similar developments.

To gain full advantage of using metrics they were monitored and reported regularly, and used as a basis of assessing progress and identifying problems as early as possible. They were used as follows:

- **Sizing metrics** - The size of the product was monitored closely at module level. If code growth occurred in the completed modules, it was an indication that the total product may be bigger than anticipated. This could result in changes to the cost and schedule, unless other metrics changed in a manner which would compensate for it. For example, if the product size doubled then it would take twice as long to code and unit test it unless productivity was improved. The number of test cases would double unless more effective test cases could be written, and the total number of defects would double unless quality could be improved.

- **Productivity metrics** - Constant monitoring of the productivity rates gave early warning of potential overspending and schedule slippage, allowing corrective action to be taken if possible.

- **Quality metrics** - These were also monitored for deviations and trends, allowing corrective action to be taken. This action could take the form of procedural changes, or increased inspection, or defect fixing effort.

Overall the use of metrics was very beneficial to the management team, but was viewed as unnecessary extra paperwork by some of the technical members of the team. This highlights the importance of minimizing the effort required to collect the data.

10.4 Data Logic Manufacturing Company Application

10.4.1 Application Overview

This project was undertaken for a large manufacturing company and consisted of two distinct phases. Phase one was to take an existing Business Systems Definition (BSD) and produce a Technical Design Overview document and Program Specifications. During this phase the data base design was checked for completeness and the BSD for consistency. This phase was undertaken on a Time and Materials cost basis.

Phase two followed on from Phase one and turned the previously produced Program Specifications into code. It then undertook unit, link, and system testing before handing the completed system over to the client's Business Analyst to undertake acceptance testing. This phase was handled as a Fixed Price contract. Support for error fixing was provided during the acceptance testing.

The application was a document tracking system for components of the design and manufacture of the company's product. The project undertook to add new facilities which allowed additional components to be tracked by the expanded computer system. The new functionality had to work in the same manner as existing programs and interface to much of the existing functionality.

The project developed 84 programs, a small number of which

were modifications to existing programs. The end result was the generation of approximately 40,000 lines of code (LOC). The LOC was measured as Procedure Division statements minus comments. The majority of the programs implemented on-line dialogs.

The production environment for the developed system was an IBM mainframe running under the MVS operating system. The programs were written in COBOL and the on-line dialogs used CICS. The data base used in this environment was IMS/DB (DL/1).

The development environment was based on a Local Area Network (LAN) of IBM-compatible PCs. The network ran on the client's twisted-pair wiring using Novell Netware and was linked to the mainframe via a gateway. All the documentation was produced using WordPerfect 5.1, including the Program Specifications, Test Plans, and all reporting. The programmers used the Micro Focus Workbench product to develop and unit test the code. A limited amount of link testing was possible on the LAN, however the majority was carried out on the mainframe following migration. The System Testing was carried out on the mainframe, by a team separate from the main development teams.

The entire project was carried out at the client site and involved a number of client staff. There were a number of reasons for this, not least the inexperience of the client staff with respect to the network-based products. The client wished to gain some practical experience and benefit from technology transfer, prior to making the final decision about a move to using the network-based development technology themselves.

10.4.2 Development Process

The various stages that were undertaken during the project reflected the normal Data Logic Systems Development Life-Cycle (SDLC).

- Functional Requirements Specification
- Functional Specification
- Design (Technical) Specification
- Development (Program Specification, Coding, Unit and Link Testing)

- System Testing
- Acceptance Testing.

This project started at the Design (Technical) Specification stage. However, in order to ensure that the size/shape of the task was agreed to in advance, the Technical Design stage was preceded by a short review of all the existing documentation, primarily the BSD. The staff on the team were also briefed concerning the deliverables required and the document format to be used. The document format was agreed to and signed off by the client.

A Quality Plan was produced. This described the manner in which the project was to be undertaken; i.e., the detailed processes and procedures. This document was discussed with and subsequently issued to the client.

A detailed project plan was set up using Project Manager Workbench (PMW), and progress was then monitored on a weekly basis. This monitoring and any subsequently updated dates for deliverables followed the approach described by the Data Logic Project Control System (PCS). The project was also tracked by a senior Data Logic manager who was independent of the project.

All deliverables, documents, designs, test plans, and code were reviewed by members of the team. Any errors detected were recorded and their correction tracked to completion. A selected number of each type of deliverable were formally inspected by a team of people which included a quality representative. A formal report of any errors was produced and the resolution of the errors was tracked. The aim was to inspect deliverables from all project staff as early in the project as possible.

Once the project team was satisfied with the deliverables they were given to the client's Business Analyst. The deliverables were signed off by the Business Analyst following resolution of any errors he found.

During the development stage, the coding and unit testing were controlled by the various team leaders. They were responsible for reviewing all program designs, test plans, code, and test results. They also provided technical assistance, support, and guidance to the less experienced members of the team. Where possible, this was handled by other more experienced members of the team. This was extremely important in the early stages, especially where the client's staff were involved.

The system-testing stage was controlled by a team leader who was independent of the development teams. The system test team leader generated the system test plan and also managed the staff who fixed any errors detected during system testing.

The acceptance test stage was carried out by the client's Business Analyst against the BSD. Any errors detected at this stage were resolved by the support programmers, and when they had all been resolved the client representative signed off the system as accepted.

10.4.3 Metrics Used

10.4.3.1 Phase One

During Phase one the main metrics used were:

- Errors identified per deliverable document
- Type of errors
- Status of document.

The details collected were analyzed in order to provide feedback for future projects about the total number of errors and the effort to fix. More importantly the number of outstanding errors and the status of various documents were used to demonstrate that progress towards resolving all errors, and completing the documents, was being made.

10.4.3.2 Phase Two

During Phase two the main metrics were:

- LOC generated
  - per day
  - per program
  - per dialog
  - for the entire project.

The LOC numbers collected and the effort necessary to produce the various programs were used to provide input to the company's guidelines. The values were averages; i.e., final size divided by the time taken, not daily counts.

During the project it was also possible to determine which individuals were suffering from any learning curve problems, and which programs were turning out to be different in terms of complexity/size when compared to how they were perceived during estimation and planning. It was necessary to understand the complexity of the program, the possibility/practicality of reusing code from elsewhere, before making judgments about performance as opposed to productivity. When a new program was little different from an existing program on which it could be based, productivity levels were very high. For example, in these circumstances a 500-line program could be generated, tested, and documented in less than a day.

When a program continued to grow and the number of outstanding errors remained constant or grew, then a problem was identified which in some cases resulted in the program being rewritten from scratch. The need to start again, or any other appropriate remedial action, was determined following an in-depth review of the program with all appropriate staff.

The productivity and completion trends based on the performance of the whole team and particular groups of staff working on similar sets of programs, were used to assist in forecasting when development would actually be completed.

Metrics which were tracked on errors included:

- Errors identified per program during
    - development/unit test
    - system test
    - acceptance test
- Type of errors - severity.

The main benefit of collecting the metrics related to errors and the severity of the errors was to demonstrate to the client that the quality of the overall deliverable was being controlled and could be seen to be improving. The accuracy of information collected at the unit testing stage was always open to question, and this was only used to help to determine whether a problem existed. The collection of error metrics related to System Test and Acceptance were more useful. The trends in terms of errors being identified over time and the number of outstanding errors indicated whether progress through the phase was being made. The severity of the errors identified was the main determining factor for prioritizing the order in which they would be fixed. The improving trends for individuals, groups, and the whole team demonstrated increased familiarity with the application, more experience with the environment, and adherence to the processes/procedures. From the client's point of view this was most vividly demonstrated by the fact that the Business Analyst found only one critical error during Acceptance Testing.

Metrics associated with correction effort included:

- Effort necessary to resolve errors.

During System and Acceptance Testing not only were the errors formally logged, but the effort to fix each error was recorded. Thus projections of outstanding required effort/resources could be made. In this project the errors identified were batched together and accurate individual error fix times were not always available. The fact that the errors were normally being closed more quickly than they were being found meant that there were very few outstanding errors at any given time. The total effort to fix the errors was costed and this amount then became one component of the cost of quality.

For the whole project, additional metrics that were used included:

- Effort Days planned vs. Effort Days used

- Planned cost vs. Actual cost.

The contract with the client was written in such a way that the use of System Variation Requests (SVRs), i.e. changes to the requirements which resulted in more effort/cost, was excluded. In order to fit within the time-scale and budget which had been agreed and presented to the ultimate end-users it was therefore necessary to negotiate over the scope of the system. The functionality which was to be delivered was therefore prioritized so that everyone was clear on the size/shape of the elements which could be left out, if necessary. The quality of the BSD and the initial review was such that this situation only arose once and was quickly and amicably resolved. The importance of the PCS in collecting the above metrics was essential in having quantitative values on which the agreements could be based. The overall size of the system in terms of LOC was also a useful indicator during these negotiations. From the Data Logic point of view it also meant that the profitability (margin) of the project could also be tracked.

10.4.4 Quality Improvement Techniques

The main techniques/procedures used to ensure the required level of quality in the deliverables were:

- Inspections
- Tracking
- SEI Evaluation/Audit
- Termination Report.

All these techniques/procedures consisted of a number of components, and they provided a number of benefits both at the project and company levels.

10.4.4.1 Inspections

The different approaches ranged from informal reviews by other team members to formal reviews by a group, comprised of both team members and individuals independent from the project.

10.4.4.1.1 Peer Reviews

These were carried out by individuals with some understanding of the system and were often the first stage of assessment for a deliverable. Sometimes this was the only assessment. Errors found were documented, and the generator of the deliverable then corrected the errors and demonstrated to the Team Leader that the corrections had been successfully completed.

10.4.4.1.2 Walkthroughs

In this situation the deliverable was reviewed as above except that the generator of the deliverable presented and discussed the content with the Team Leader. He was then advised as to which changes were required. This was a much more interactive form of review.

10.4.4.1.3 Formal Inspections

The approach here was very much more formal with all participants reviewing the deliverable, documenting their comments, and then attending a meeting at which all significant points were discussed and resolved. The changes arising out of this process were tracked to resolution. The amended deliverable was subsequently checked by the appointed individual, normally the moderator (who was also empowered to decide between any differences of opinion), and then signed off.

At least one deliverable from each of the generators was inspected, as early in the appropriate phase as possible. This ensured that any errors detected were resolved as soon as possible, but more importantly that errors which affected all generators were communicated so that they were not repeated by each individual.

As the project progressed and the staff learned from the queries raised during earlier inspections, it was possible to reduce the number of inspections that were carried out. The quality of the documents/deliverables produced following this decision was maintained. The full-time involvement of the team leaders and active participation of the project management in all the above ensured a common understanding which was maintained throughout the project.

10.4.4.2 Tracking

The Project Initiation meeting was in effect Tracking meeting Zero, and it ensured that the contracted business was understood and that the required resources were available and trained. The subsequent meetings were chaired by an independent senior manager from within the organization, who was charged with reviewing the status of the project and advising on any issues/problems encountered. The tracking process reported to the company management, and it reviewed the project from a commercial and legal perspective.

10.4.4.3 SEI Evaluation/Audit

This procedure was carried out several months into the project. By completing the SEI evaluation questionnaire the project manager was in effect performing a self-audit of the project. Discussion with the auditor answered any ambiguous or unclear questions. The results of the analysis of the answers to the questions gave an overall maturity level indicator (not that useful on its own) and an assessment, using the questions which were not positively answered, of the areas for improvement. The areas evaluated by the questions included the procedures, documentation, reporting, and feedback given to staff. The analysis indicated where these areas were satisfactorily in place, where they were not in place and changes were necessary, and where they were not in place and changes could have been beneficial.

This project was assessed as having a maturity level of 2. There were only a small number of questions which prevented it from reaching level 3. Where these negative responses were also significant from a BS5750 point of view, the processes/procedures were modified.

10.4.4.4 Termination Report

The Termination Report was produced very near the end of the project, and it contributed to the improvement of Data Logic's approach to running projects by:

- Identifying problems encountered and describing how they were overcome.

- Describing lessons learned from the above and successes in the way the project was run. This included techniques for training, technology transfer, working on site, and integration of client staff.

- Summarizing the actual time and cost compared with the planned time and cost. Identifying why there were any differences and how they arose, plus what had changed during the project. This information was important for the process of continually trying to improve the estimates, so that clients could have a greater degree of certainty over both cost and time-scales.

10.4.5 Benefits

The client objectives for the project were:

- To deliver an agreed system on schedule and
- To ensure that the delivered system was high quality.

Therefore, the aim of the metrics used was to assist in identifying the completeness and the quality of the deliverables. The information collected also allowed the project manager to predict the effort required to complete the deliverables to the required level of quality.

During Phase one, reviews and inspections ensured that consistent high-quality documents were produced. They adhered to the agreed format, were complete, and accurately reflected the functionality being described. Reporting on progress, including error resolution, also gave the client a high level of confidence in the quality of the documents being produced.

The involvement of the client's representatives at all stages, including reviews, progress meetings, and the development and testing, meant that there were few misunderstandings with regard to the functionality being developed.

During Phase two, it was possible to monitor the performance of individuals and teams, in order to identify areas where programs might be more difficult than originally estimated. This helped to determine programs/dialogs which might require additional testing, or where additional resources or a formal inspection might ensure that problems were identified and subsequently resolved as early as possible.

The overall values of LOC/day for the project and errors detected at various stages helped to demonstrate the continuing improvement in the quality of the system. These also provided valuable feedback into the company's estimating guidelines. The client was able to use the numbers to demonstrate in a quantified, objective way that productivity was considerably higher than normally achieved using the mainframe (on this project twice what would have been expected). Additionally, the only lost time from the LAN-based development environment was a general power failure on the site, and some delay while one of the printers was repaired. This compared well with the mainframe users' contention and unavailability problems.

Finally, client confidence was high throughout the project and the number of surprises was greatly reduced.

11 Best Practices and Benefits Experience - ETNOTEAM

11.1 Software Maintenance Product Assessment

11.1.1 Application Overview

ETNOTEAM Spa is a privately-owned Italian software company with approximately 180 employees that was founded in 1978. ETNOTEAM is strongly connected with the educational and research activities of the University of Milano. The company is located in Milan with an operating subsidiary in Rome. ETNOTEAM is involved with custom software development and consulting on software engineering for large industries and banks.

The practice described in this section will be referred to as 'product check-up'. It is a consultant-oriented practice performed by ETNOTEAM aimed at the analysis of delivered software products for which maintenance activities are being carried out. Its purpose is to evaluate the product in order to:

- compare its actual performance with the specified performance with respect to quality factors such as: maintainability, portability, interoperability, usability, efficiency, reliability, correctness, and verifiability;

- determine the critical areas in the product;

- propose the best evolution strategy, i.e.:

  . ordinary maintenance

  . re-engineering

. reverse engineering

. restructuring

. throw-away and re-development.

A 'context diagram' showing the main external interfaces of the method is given in Figure 11.1.

This section provides examples of practices that are used for phase metrics for a product in the maintenance phase.

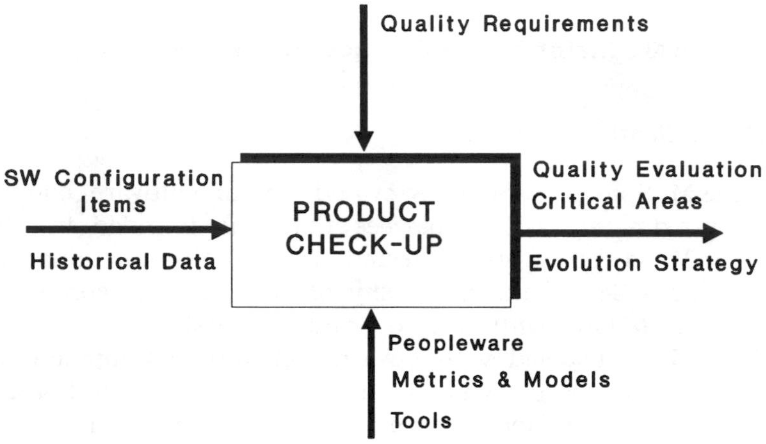

Figure 11.1 Product Check-Up Method.

11.1.2 Product Check-Up Method

The overall method can be performed as an internal activity of a software development unit having particular skills in software metrics and models, or by cooperation between a software development unit and a team of expert consultants. The method can also be applied within an 'off-the-shelf' service provided by a 'quality assessment laboratory'. The laboratory obtains the product software configuration items and historical data, and then provides a 'check-up' report. This is done after having agreed to the quality factors to inspect, and having analyzed the product by means of its own experts and tools.

The method is composed of six main steps (Figure 11.2).

1. Survey of the method;
2. Selection of quality factors to be assessed;
3. Selection of software items to be inspected;
4. Application of metrics and checklists;
5. Evaluation of critical aspects;
6. Proposal for an evolution strategy.

A brief overview of each step is given below.

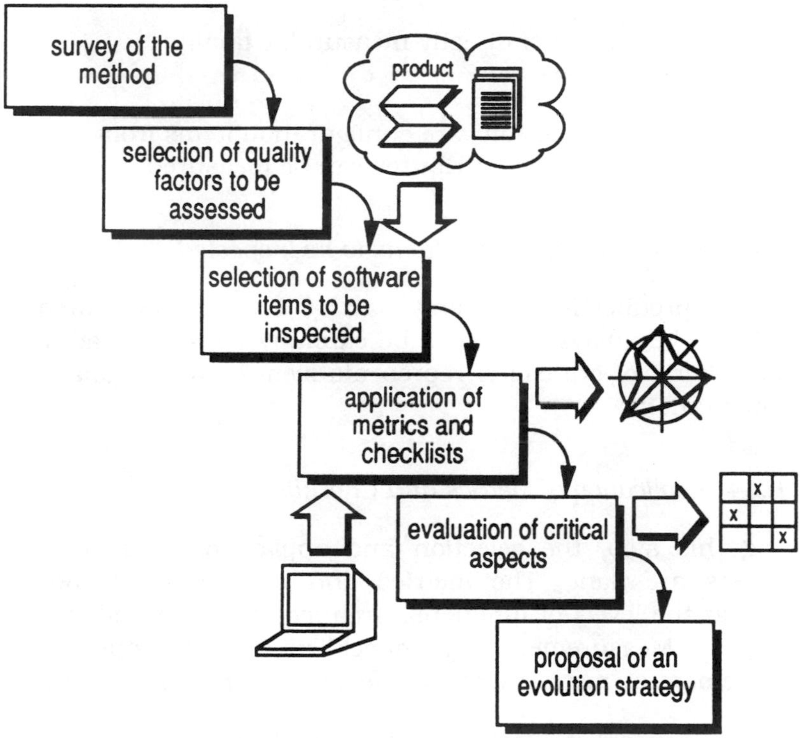

Figure 11.2 Product Check-Up Method Steps.

11.1.2.1 Survey of the Method

This preliminary step is needed when the application of the method requires a cooperative effort between the software developers and the assessment team. In this case, the assessment team describes the goals to be achieved, and the methods to be utilized.

11.1.2.2 Selection of Quality Factors to be Assessed

This activity aims at defining the key relevant quality factors among the ones of a predefined quality model. In particular, the following actions are performed:

- selection of relevant quality factors from a user's point of view;
- derivation of directly measurable quality attributes;
- selection of software configuration items from which quality attributes can be measured.

11.1.2.3 Selection of Software Items to be Inspected

When the product is large, only part of it will be evaluated. The samples to be analyzed have to be carefully chosen, in adherence to the criteria of criticality, representativeness, and availability of documentation.

11.1.2.4 Application of Metrics and Checklists

During this step, the selection and application of metrics and checklists are done. The metrics and checklists are normally applied at the levels of functions, architecture, code and evolution history. Measurement by checklists is as objective as measurement by metrics when the following conditions are met:

- checklist questions are well defined;
- checklist questions are weighted (optional);
- the answers to checklist questions belong to a predefined range of values.

In this case a final 'objective' measure can in fact be obtained as a function of the checklist answers, typically in the form of a weighted sum.

The application of metrics and checklists is not evenly applied on all chosen configuration items; instead, the analysis area is further refined by means of the following strategy.

- building a high-level model of the product (i.e., by means of Petri Nets or structured methodologies such as SA, SD, SA/RT, SADT, etc.);

- comparison of the model with the known environment reality, and subsequent determination of critical areas. This stages relies on the hypothesis that the maintenance of a software product is heavily dependent on its 'isomorphism' to the real field of application;

- analysis of the architecture and the code implementing the previously identified critical areas (application of metrics and checklists);

- analysis of error trend and distribution (statistical analysis);

- analysis of the architecture and the code implementing the previously identified error-prone areas (application of metrics and checklists).

11.1.2.5 Evaluation of Critical Aspects

During this step, results coming from measurements are integrated, in order to have feedback on quality attributes (technical view) and quality factors (user's view). The evaluation at various integration levels may consist of:

- checks for predefined pass/fail criteria;

- usage of a positioning matrix enhancing the readability of differences between specified and actual performance.

The matrix combines the relevance and the evaluation of each attribute; the attributes with high relevance and low evaluation are to be considered critical.

11.1.2.6 Proposal for an Evolution Strategy

This step tries to synthesize symptoms going from diagnosis toward therapy, taking into account the following parameters:

- Cost-Benefit Tradeoff: This parameter can be evaluated considering that each symptom is associated to a list of tasks to be performed, along with the resulting benefits in terms of maintenance effort reduction. The software development unit can then estimate the cost for each task, and compare it with the expected benefit.

- Reliability of Actual Service: This parameter is a function of error trend and user satisfaction.

- The possibility for the product to withstand further functional maintenance.

- The maturity of hardware and software technologies used.

The application of a decision-table combining the above-mentioned parameters together with the possible evolution strategies concludes this step and the overall activity.

11.1.3 Metrics Used

The product check-up method is highly flexible. As a consequence, metrics and checklists to be used are strongly dependent on the software product to be assessed. The choice is determined by:

- the availability of appropriate documentation and automated support tools;

- the confidence of the metrics results; and

- the level of knowledge of the data providers.

Quite often, a need for new metrics or checklists arises. In those cases, the definition of the metrics or checklist is done in accordance with the goal-directed methodology (called Goals/Questions/Metrics) for collecting valid software engineering data, developed at the Software Engineering Laboratory by Professor Basili's team (Basili, 1984).

The selection of specific metrics is dependent on the extensive expertise of the assessment team, and their ability to choose metrics that will be easily understood by the software maintainer's management and staff. As stated above, the metrics will characterize the product quality at functional, architecture, code, and evolution history levels.

11.1.4 Quality Improvement Techniques

In order to improve the readability of results and their analysis several kinds of tools are used:

- CASE tools for model building and evaluation
- Static analyzers
- Checklist managers
- Data analysis tools.

The above tools provide various tables, diagrams, and data views, such as:

- call graphs, to evaluate the complexity and the structure of the low-level architecture
- control graphs, to evaluate the complexity and the structure of the algorithms
- Kiviat diagrams, to synthesize the results of the evaluation of the various metrics
- bar and pie charts, to analyze trends and dynamic information.

The interpretation of results to form business strategy recommendations requires extensive consulting expertise and experience. The goal is to facilitate readability and easy assimilation of the results for the benefit of the maintainer's management and staff. Several forms of graphical output for trends analysis and historical information are used.

Analysis on data is done at many different levels (on simple data sets, selected classes of data sets, all the data, etc.). All analyses are based upon simple statistical indices.

In Figure 11.3, an example of error distribution for an actual project is shown. An examination of the fault distribution data (frequency of faults in field use by release) reveals the following:

i. upon issue of a release, a jump in the number of faults is observed;

ii. for releases subsequent to release 3, the number of faults increases sharply. This is indicative of problems encountered within the maintenance activity.

Examining the architecture of the product confirms that at this point, the structure deteriorated quite badly, due to the various maintenance activities. In fact, given this situation, the recommendation to management at this point, was to 'throw away and redevelop' the product.

11.1.5 Benefits

The impact of the product check-up practice is threefold:

- at the organizational level, it provides a precise guideline to follow, assuring that the overall method is non-biased, efficient, and cost effective;

- at the project level, it helps in clarifying in detail the functional and structural aspects of the product and greatly improves the traceability of the software configuration items;

- at the economics level, it helps to plan activities in advance, to forecast costs, and it substantially reduces the effort involved in deciding what is to be modified and how it should be modified.

The practice has shown that the method is valuable for effective management of the evolution of existing software products. The method has proven to be applicable on most kinds of software systems. In particular, it has been applied in the fields of telecommunications, real-time systems, operating systems, 'off-the-shelf' commercial products, large information systems, and others.

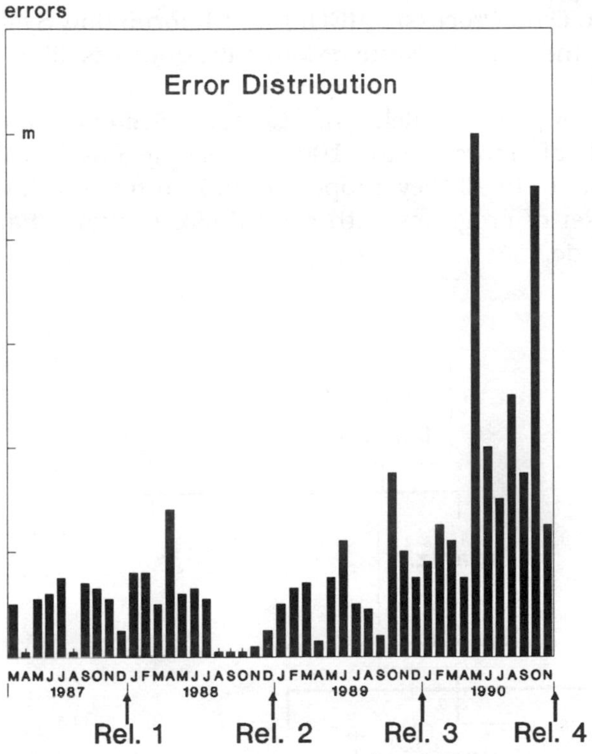

Figure 11.3 Example Error Distribution.

11.2 Quality System Introduction

11.2.1 Application Overview

This section describes experience with the introduction of a software quality system, and the metrics that were introduced to measure the effectiveness of the new development practices.

11.2.1.1 Environment

The successful experience described in this section is related to the introduction of a Quality System for software development in a large Italian bank. The modified development environment incorporates the use of a small number of metrics which enables better evaluation of costs and benefits.

The organization of the bank is shown in Figure 11.4. The Electronic Data Processing (EDP) and Information System function in which the Quality System was introduced is illustrated in the figure.

The group for which the Quality System was introduced consisted of more than 100 people involved with software development. In all they supported an Information System consisting of a set of programs with a total size of more than 12 million lines of code.

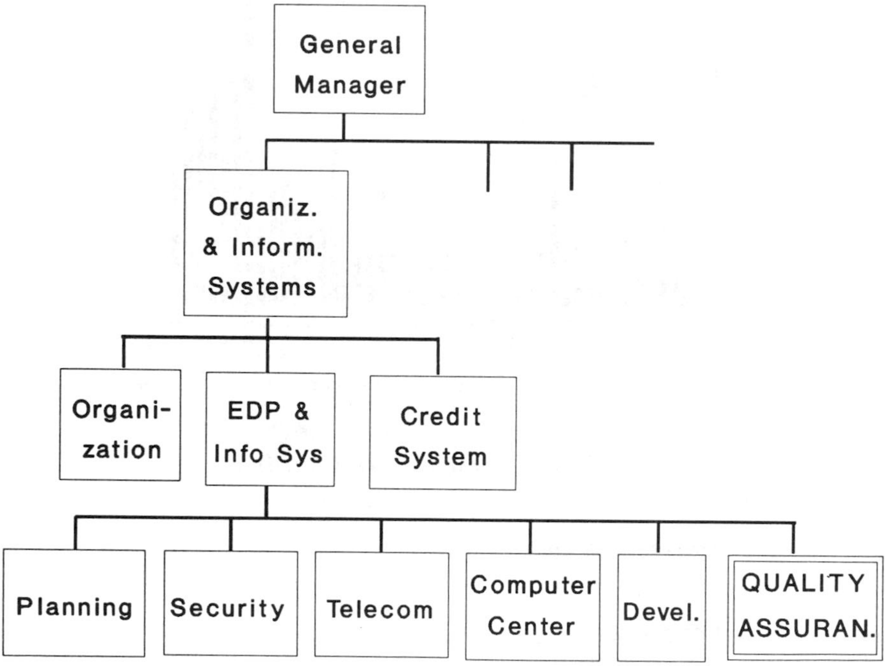

Figure 11.4 Bank Organization.

11.2.1.2 Objectives

The initial status of the group was characterized by:

- weak development organization;
- presence of a software development methodology framework that was not uniformly applied;
- very limited Quality Control activities.

The Quality System Introduction Program had the following objectives:

- to establish good practices of software development (Organization, Methods, and Tools) in a controlled environment;
- to introduce specific formal review and testing activities, with measurements of the amount of Quality Control effort performed;
- to measure the effects of the changes introduced on quality and productivity.

In particular, the following activities were introduced.

- A Quality Manual was developed defining roles, responsibilities, organization, procedures for software planning, development, verification and validation, and configuration management. The structure of this Quality Manual is given below.

  . principles
    ... purpose of the manual
    ... definition of the software product structure in terms of its major functional components
    ... control and evolution of the Quality System
  . norms
    ... roles and responsibilities
    ... software life-cycle
    ... software documentation and related life-cycle

... risk classes and Quality Plan
... Verification and Validation (V&V) activities
. procedures
... testing
... configuration management and release
... Non conformity (Deviation) management
... purchasing software.

- The concept of Risk Class was defined as an attribute of every application, related to a 'quality profile'. This is a vector ranking the required presence of the software quality attributes as taken from a well-known quality model (Arthur, 1984). Questionnaires were set up for determining the proper quality profile of an application.

- A Quality Plan was introduced as an initial development project document. The purpose of the Quality Plan is for tailoring the Quality Manual requirements on the specific project for the defined risk class. This helps to determine the most relevant project documents and V&V activities dependent on the quality profile.

- V&V practices, and in particular systematic functional testing and formal reviews (based on standard checklists), were introduced and widely applied.

11.2.2 Metrics Used

The metrics used in the evaluation of the improvements are very simple and easy to collect. They are:

- The costs in man-days spent on a project for the various activities:

  - development

  - V&V activities

... reviews

.... on the various documents

... testing

.... on the various phases

- maintenance.

- The quantity of software maintenance performed. This is measured as the number of delivered 'objects' (compilation units) that were changed for maintenance. This measure has been chosen as a rough estimation of the 'external quality' of the products. Historically it was observed that in the initial years after delivery, many objects were changed for removing problems. That is, modifications were made for setting up the products and tuning them, and not for their functional evolution (Figure 11.5).

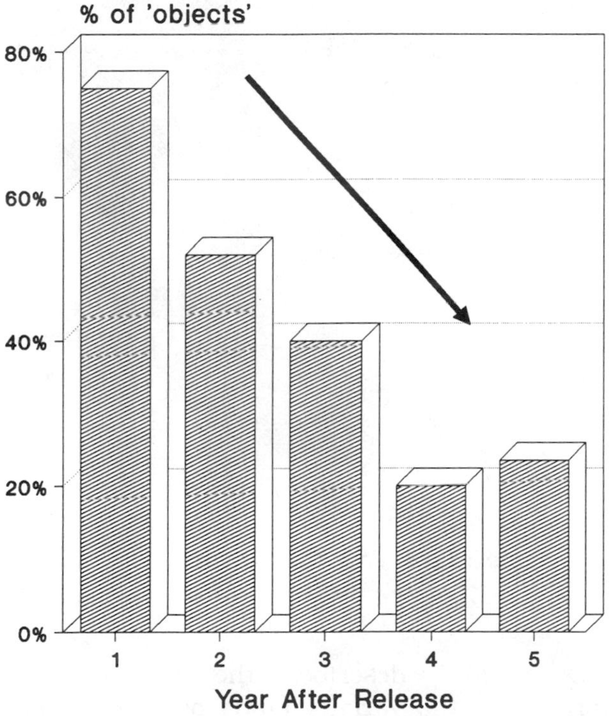

Figure 11.5 Trends in Changes (Observed without V&V).

11.2.3 Usefulness of Metrics - Lessons Learned

The metrics applied provided high confidence in the cost distribution of the quality-control activities. Summarized information is given in the following figures:

- Figure 11.6 shows that the testing costs were more than three times the costs for the reviews.

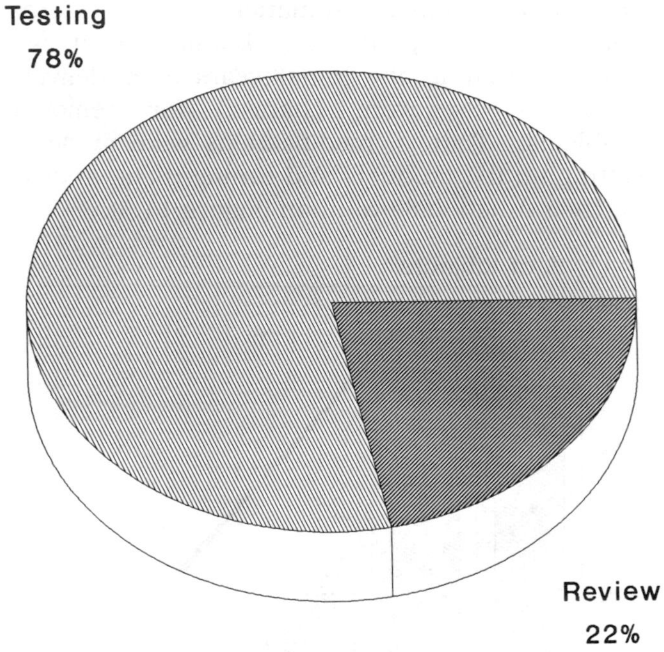

Figure 11.6 V&V Cost Distribution.

- Figure 11.7 describes the review effort performed on the various kinds of development documents, indicating the high degree of attention given to design documents.

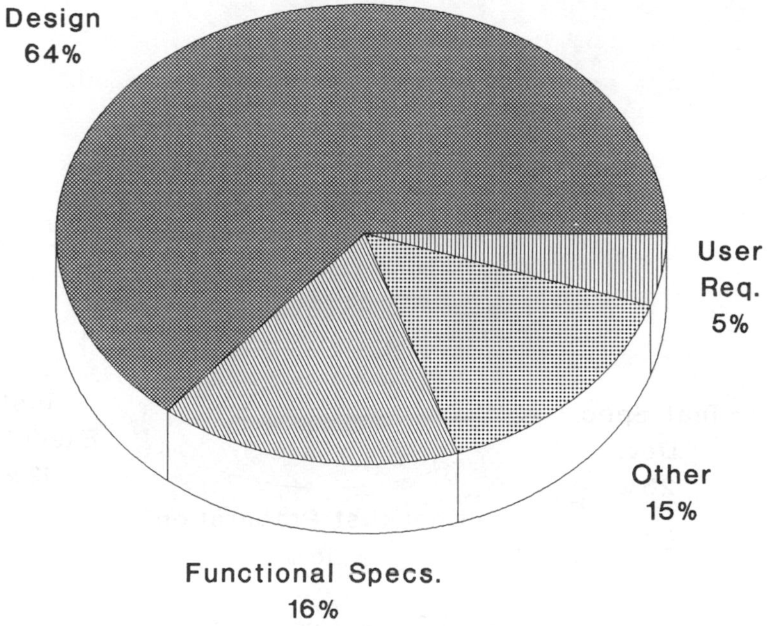

Figure 11.7 Review Cost Distribution.

- Figure 11.8 shows the distribution of testing efforts, following a methodology in which the steps were:

  - product analysis and test strategy definition

  - checklist preparation; i.e., the ordered systematic collection of the functional item to be tested, extracted from the product functional specification

  - test specification and development (including input data construction and expected result description)

  - test execution

  - launch report examination and quality report production.

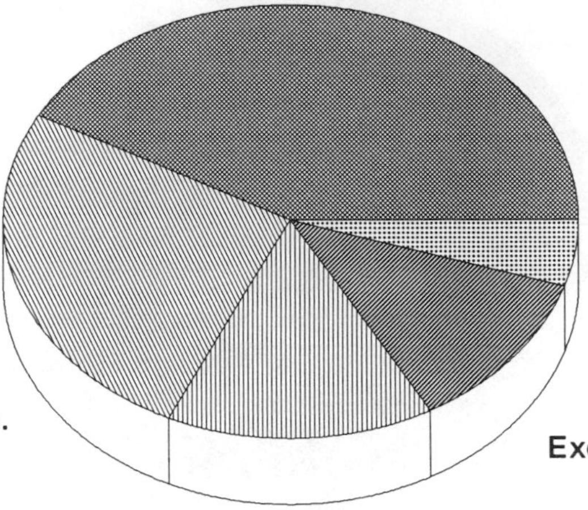

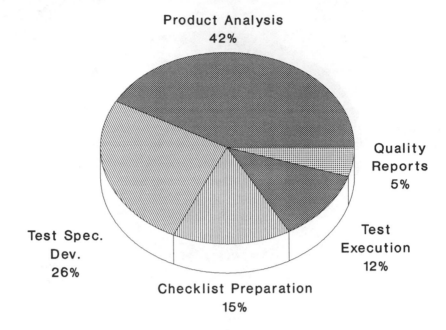

Figure 11.8 Test Cost Distribution.

The collection of data using the described metrics and the results for some projects carried on in the last two years, allowed the comparison of the total cost distribution for software development, quality control, and maintenance, to projects where no quality control was systematically performed. The results are shown in Figure 11.9, in which we see that:

- The introduction of V&V activities introduces additional effort which is almost 20% of the development costs.

- The development staff estimated that maintenance costs were at least 50% of overall life-cycle costs prior to the introduction of V&V activities. The effect of these V&V activities during development was to reduce the maintenance costs to 60% of the maintenance costs of projects implemented prior to the V&V activities.

- The net saving on the total costs is close to 20% of the development costs; i.e., 10% of the total amount spent for software development and maintenance.

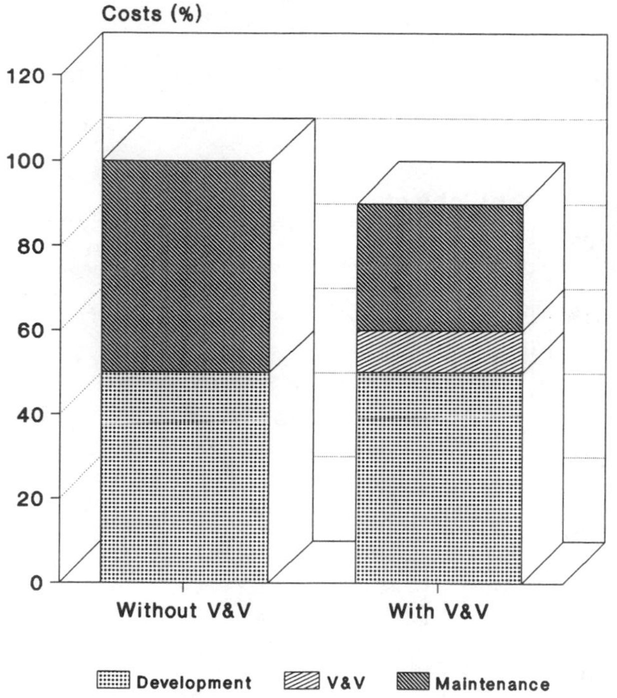

Figure 11.9 Quality Practices Benefits.

Examining the data for projects carried out with the newly introduced V&V techniques, we found that the software maintenance trends seem to have changed (Figure 11.10). Even taking into account that the data gathered is still limited and that it covers a relatively short time-scale, it seems that newly released products are already initially more stable. They require significantly less maintenance upon release. The need for maintenance subsequently increases in time rather than decreases. This is a positive trend if we recognize that the changes required are not corrections to faults, but evolving enhancements to functionality. They reflect changes in the operational environment which the software continues to model successfully upon modification. Thus the maintenance activity resources can be applied more to product enhancements rather than fault correction.

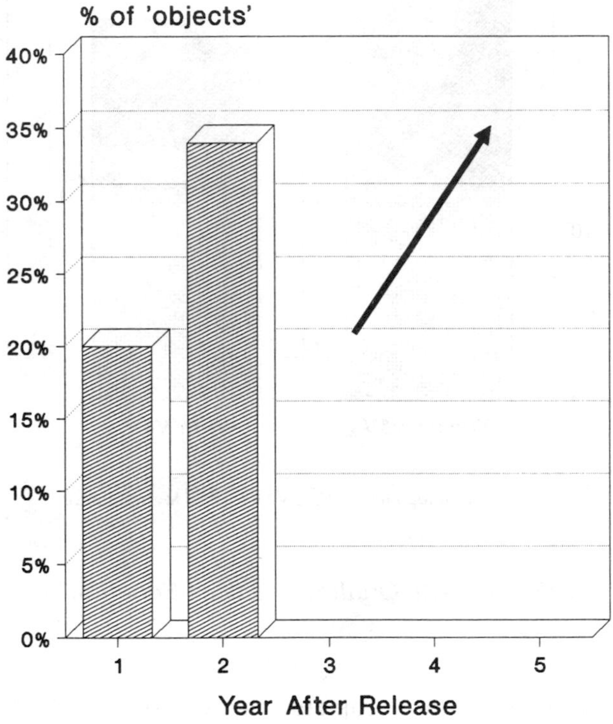

Figure 11.10 Trends in Changes with V&V.

12 VERIDATAS Code Inspection Metrics

12.1 Introduction

VERIDATAS is a French company established in 1986 involved with consulting in the areas of software engineering, quality assurance, and process certification. VERIDATAS, which consists of approximately sixty employees, is a wholly-owned subsidiary of BUREAU VERITAS. BUREAU VERITAS, which was founded in 1828, is involved with consulting in the areas of system quality and safety.

This chapter describes a simple use of phase metrics set up by VERIDATAS to solve one of its customer's problems using code inspections.

This chapter consists of three parts:

- The first part describes the problem. It describes the industrial and technical background of the VERIDATAS consultation, and then it explains the precise problem to be solved.

- The second part describes the solution used.

- The third and last part describes the practical implementation and results of this practice.

12.2 Problem Description

12.2.1 Industrial Background

VERIDATAS is heavily involved in software quality assurance (QA) consulting, and is also assisting its clients in performing various software quality assurance tasks in cooperation with the client.

In this particular case, the VERIDATAS client is the quality assurance department of a large buyer of software which receives software packages from multiple sources.

Among the various QA tasks performed, software code inspection is used extensively because of its efficiency in detecting problems. The results of the inspections are twofold:

- An immediate result is obtained by means of problem reports which lead to further detailed investigation and to fault correction.

- A longer term result is continuous quality monitoring of the various suppliers of software.

The quantitative approach set up in this case aims at assisting the second result.

12.2.2 Technical Background

The programs to be inspected consist of an average of approximately 100 procedures with a range between 30 and 250 procedures. The procedures belong to four different classes. Each of these classes is inspected using different criteria.

The programs are inspected on a sampling basis; i.e., not all of the procedures are inspected. Nevertheless, the ratio of procedures that are inspected is fairly high (40%).

The inspections are conducted using checklists. Four different checklists are used corresponding to the four different classes of procedures.

The checklists consist of approximately thirty questions relating to six characteristics of the procedure:

- header

- declaration zone

- control graph and metrics provided by a static code analyzer

- general presentation of the code

- structure of the code

- data aspects.

The checklist questions are of a binary nature, and the possible answers are: yes, no, and not applicable. The answers are directly collected on the checklists, but whenever serious anomalies are encountered, special reports are filled out using special forms.

The questions on the checklists are further linked to the following six quality attributes:

- self-description
- completeness
- coherence
- simplicity
- traceability
- modularity.

Each question is linked to only one quality attribute.

12.2.3 Problem to be Solved

The problem to be solved concerns the automatic derivation of quality indicators to enable the monitoring of problem quality. This is to be accomplished:

- among the various suppliers of software;
- among different software packages from the same supplier.

The metrics are derived from the code inspection checklists.

12.3 Solution

Two types of quality indicators are used:

- The number of serious anomalies in a program, and their rate (e.g. number of serious remarks per procedure);

- Synthetic indicators pertaining to the six quality attributes identified above in Section 12.2.2.

The first indicator is straightforward, but it is difficult to use for precise quality monitoring.

The second type of indicator is created to give a synthetic view on the program quality from the perspective of the six quality attributes. The basic inputs for these metrics are the number of 'no's' on the checklists, with a weighting factor which represents the impact of each question on the quality criteria. This weighting factor is an integer value from 1 to 4.

The quality attribute per criteria is then defined as given below.

> The quality attribute for criteria *c* is calculated as the sum of all the weighting factors for each checklist question answered with 'no' divided by the sum of all weighting factors for each inspected procedure for all questions linked to criteria *c*.

These attributes are then expressed in percentages with '0%' being best and '100%' worst. This scale was chosen to preserve compatibility with the client's practices which always relate quality to the number of discovered defects. A reverse scale could be easily designed by using the number of 'yes' answers as the basic inputs.

A table is then produced which indicates the calculated quality attribute (0-100%) for all inspected procedures for each quality attribute. An average value for all inspected procedures is then calculated for each quality attribute. An overall index is then calculated for the program by calculating the average value for the six quality attributes. An example quality attribute table is given in Figure 12.1.

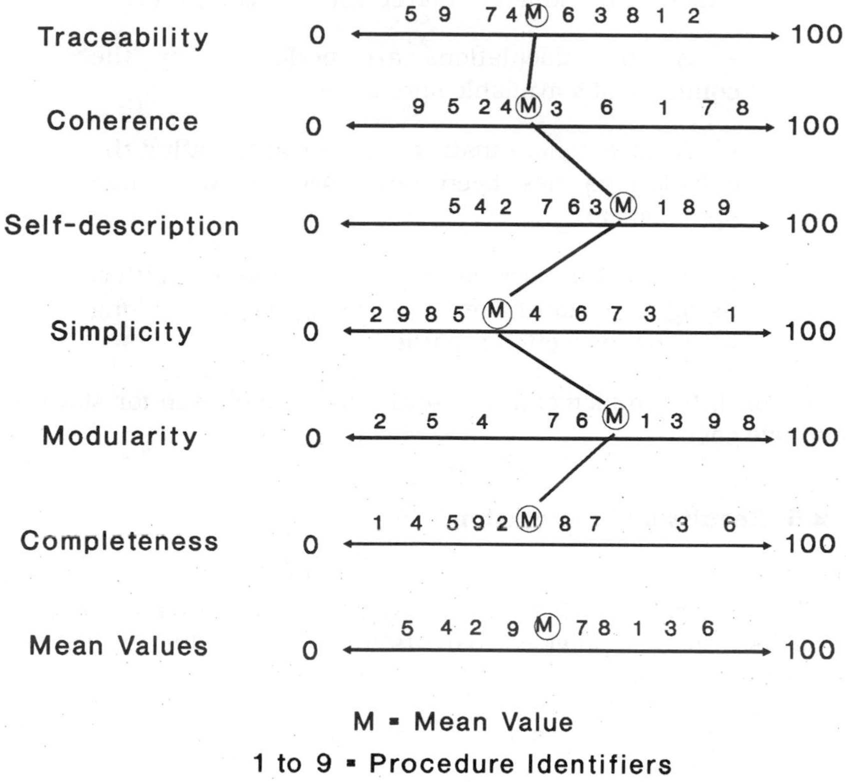

Figure 12.1 Example Quality Attribute Table.

12.4 Implementation

This system has been used by VERIDATAS for the client. It is presently implemented as follows:

- The checklists are created using a commercially available spreadsheet package on Macintosh computers.

- During the code inspections, the checklists are either directly filled in by electronic form, or by paper form and later entered into the computer.

- All the calculations are performed by the commercially available spreadsheet.

- A set of macro-instructions for automating the calculations has been developed on the same spreadsheet.

- The results are edited on the same computer, using a standard word processing package, along with the inspection reports.

In general, the implementation solutions were chosen for simplicity and low cost.

12.5 Results and Conclusion

This chapter describes a simple technique that is used for evaluating code quality during inspections. After only a few months of use, it provided insights for implementing the following quality improvements:

- design rules were revised and new ones are now used;

- an automated tool for updating the list of variables in the headers was implemented and is now used;

- a new tool to monitor the range of values of variables has been designed and implemented.

In accordance with the feedback principle used in implementing metrics, the checklists and weighting factors for the answers have evolved twice to follow the improvement of the code design process.

13 RW-TÜV Process Monitoring System Testing

13.1 Application Overview

This chapter describes some of the practices used for developing a process monitoring system which is classified as safety-critical. The project is approximately the following size:

hardware development	1-2	staff-years
software development	2	staff-years

The software for this system consists of approximately 20,000 lines of code. The software system consists of three subsystems, two of which are safety-critical.

The practices described are concerned with phase metrics for test coverage during the testing phase.

13.2 Development Process

The project plan consists of the software development phases given below. The percentage of the total effort applied to each phase is given in parentheses.

- Requirements Definition (5.0%)
- Requirements Specification (10.0%)
- High-Level Design (5.0%)
- Detailed Design (26.5%)
- Coding/Module Test (29.0%)

- SW Integration (11.0%)
- HW/SW Integration (10.0%)
- Installation/Acceptance (3.5%)

13.3 Metrics Used

The short-term goal of this metrics application was to assist the software quality specialists in uncovering potential critical quality trouble points for each phase of the software development process.

The long-term goal of this metrics application was to create knowledge and experience for subsequent metrics applications under cost/benefit constraints. This was intended to:

- accumulate experience with data collection procedures;
- highlight connections between the metrics and process and project data.

Both Product and Test Coverage Metrics were collected.

- *Product Metrics* were calculated from the documents of the detailed design with the assistance of the DEMETER (**DE**sign **MET**rics **E**valuato**R**) tool, and from the C source code using the QUALIGRAPH tool (SzKI, Budapest, Hungary).
- *Test Coverage Metrics* were collected by using the tool S-TCAT/C (Software Research Associates). In nearly all software units, 100% branch coverage (i.e., the percentage of branches of the control graph executed at least once - the ***C1*** Metric) was achieved. In the units with less than 100% coverage, the tests were aborted. This was because the effort for the required simulators in these units was believed to be too great. For the smaller components, the ***S1*** Metric (i.e., the percentage of calls executed at least once) was collected.

Various tools and forms were used for the purpose of data collection. The collection of Error Data was the most difficult activity in the data collection process. The data was collected using change report forms. The individual changes that were made are described on the change report forms using four codes:

1. Change-Cause Code:

   F: Error rectification is the cause for the change

   O: No error is the cause for change, please explain the cause briefly

2. Error-Cause Code:

   A: Data declaration

   B: Data initialization

   C: Control flow on large scale (call of SW units)

   D: Control flow on small scale or calculation of an expression

   E: Understanding of algorithm

   F: Data flow (parameter transfer, global data used)

   G: Misunderstanding of design documents

   H: Error in design documents

   I: Environment (operating system, compiler, hardware, etc.)

   K: Clerical error

   X: Miscellaneous; please explain the cause briefly

3. Error-Discovery Code:

   Errors were discovered by:

   C: Compiler runs (various compilers)

   I: Inspection

   V: Dynamic test on host

   Z: Dynamic test on target system (HW/SW-integration)

   U: Sub-system test on target system (SW-HW/SW integration)

   G: Total system test on target system (system integration)

4. Change-Scope Code:

   Changes had to be made:

   A: In 5 or less statements

   B: In more than 5 statements within a function

   C: In 2 or more functions within a file

   D: In 2 or more files

   E: In documents of the rough design.

For the first five development phases (i.e., through Coding/Module Test), error data was also collected for inspections and walk-through using specially developed forms. These forms made possible an allocation of errors according to development phases, version number and software unit, and the errors were classified according to type.

13.4 Quality Improvement Techniques

A detailed Project Plan was prepared for the project. Resources and responsibilities were assigned to the work packages defined in the project plan.

For the two safety-critical subsystems, a Verification and Validation (V&V) Plan was generated and implemented for the individual phases. The V&V Plan defines the use of methods such as reviews, inspections, design simulation, and checklists.

For each of the first five development phases checklists were completed. The specific checklists were derived from existing masterforms and were structured according to the following quality criteria:

- completeness
- consistency
- testability
- correctness.

The checklist questions could be answered by:

- yes
- yes, plus comment/remark
- no, plus comment/remark.

The answer 'yes, plus comment/remark' was used for activities which were incomplete. These answers were summarized in a special action list and added to the checklist of the next phase.

The answer 'no' was not normally acceptable, and had to be justified in each case in order to proceed to the next phase. Any answers of 'no' resulted in a 'list of open points' for the next phase.

The software quality specialists were able to evaluate certain software quality characteristics by subjective metrics developed with the aid of checklists. These subjective metrics also aided the specialists in decision making. In addition, checklists were used in the project to make sure that sufficient measures had been undertaken to help ensure a high confidence level in the system.

Test coverage measurements (C1 and S1) were performed to show that the predefined requirements for safety-critical applications were fulfilled.

13.5 General Results and Benefits

The experience of applying checklists in the way described may be summarized as follows:

- The process of tailoring the checklists should be automated. An appropriate structure of the master checklists is essential to achieve this. This structure could be made in accordance with different quality characteristics, methods, common parts, and parts which have to be specified.

- The reusability of checklists is essential to reduce the effort in later projects.

The metrics provided by the DEMETER tool give aspects of the design, such as complexity of the modular structure of the system or interfaces. The DEMETER metrics were therefore analyzed to find out whether and which metrics are indicators for 'interface' or 'call' errors. Of specific interest is whether metrics which are simpler to calculate without the tool can provide similar system structure insights.

The metrics CO (= Number of called software units) and RP (= Number of returned parameters) supply good results with regard to the class of 'call' errors. The metrics CO and DLRE (= Design Logical Ripple Effect) give good results with regard to the class of 'interface' errors. Of particular interest is that such a 'primitive' metric as CO achieves such good results.

With regard to the class 'algorithmic' errors, nearly all complexity metrics offered by QUALIGRAPH indicate significant non-zero correlations, including the metric 'Lines of Code'.

With regard to the Test Coverage Metric, S1, only the QUALIGRAPH metric 'Accessibility' achieved significant non-zero correlations. This means that this metric is a possible indicator of the test effort required to achieve the high S1 coverage.

One of the main benefits of this metrics application was that the knowledge for later quality assurance tasks was increased. It was proved that the following tasks can be beneficially supported by metrics:

- choosing among product design alternatives;

- indicating software development process trouble points which need enhanced validation actions.

14 CRIL User Satisfaction Measurement

14.1 Environment Overview

The measurement experience described in this chapter took place in a large transport company, which has several sites in Europe, primarily in France. It provides an example of a technique for determining user satisfaction. It is an example of a phase metric for the maintenance phase. It is also an example of a technique for determining a subjective metric.

In order to track the transported goods, most of these sites have networked computing equipment. The sites are also connected with the head office, whose computers have the following roles:

- exchange of information with the clients, suppliers, and subsidiaries;
- exchange of information with the sites;
- support of clerical tasks (payroll, invoicing, etc.) and management tasks.

Many software applications run on these computers, and are used by a wide range of users, from company management to operators, who load the computers with data (data acquisition).

An Organization and Computing Department (OCD), consisting of 120 persons, is in charge of the tasks related to information management and technology. This includes management of the equipment, development, and maintenance of the software applications defined with the users, user training and support, and executing head office applications.

In 1989, the OCD decided to initiate a quality improvement process. To define quality actions and their priorities, they wished to initiate a survey to measure:

- User satisfaction concerning the applications and services provided by the OCD;

- The OCD employees' opinions regarding their interactions with the users.

The following paragraphs describe the steps of the survey definition and analysis, and the lessons learned from this experience.

14.2 Measurement Steps

The initial task consisted of the definition of the survey questionnaires and quality indicators. The next task was devoted to the analysis of the survey results.

14.2.1 Definition of Questionnaires and Quality Indicators

For this task, the Basili approach, called Goals/Questions/Metrics (Basili, 1984), was used.

The user survey questionnaires and quality indicators were first defined. The steps were as follows:

- Establish meetings with the OCD managers to learn about their goals of such a survey; i.e., what their concerns are, what information they need, etc.

- From the results of these meetings, determine the issues to be assessed, then define the goals and the survey questions.

- Validate these goals and questions with the managers, which led to refinement of the question set.

- Devise a user questionnaire, which included several types of questions; such as questions offering one choice among several (multiple-choice questions), questions asking for figures, arrays to be filled, etc.

- Test this questionnaire by having it completed by a representative sample of users. This test indicated that the questionnaire was too long, and that some of the questions and terms were not understood by some types of users.

- Define several user profiles (or populations), according to their role and workplace (e.g. head office or others).

- Create a questionnaire for each user profile, and define quality indicators corresponding to the goals.

To create the questionnaires and quality indicators for the OCD employees, the previous steps were followed, except that populations were determined at the beginning of the work, and the first set of questionnaires was directly adapted to these populations.

Having defined the questionnaires and quality indicators, the survey was conducted in mid-1990. Questionnaires were sent to about 500 users (from the head office, the sites, and the subsidiaries) and fifty employees within the OCD. The questionnaires were returned some weeks later, and the answers were then entered into a data base.

14.2.2 Survey Results Analysis

The analysis consisted of the computation of the quality indicators, and then analyzing the results.

14.2.2.1 Computation of the Quality Indicators

Each indicator was refined into sub-indicators, which could in turn be refined. We thus created two indicator trees, one for the users and the other one for the computing department staff. The root of each tree was the indicator measuring the general satisfaction or opinion, the nodes indicated the satisfaction level for an assessed issue, and the leaves were the answers to the questions of the questionnaires.

Figures of merit were assigned to each of the possible answers of the multiple-choice questions. The method to aggregate these figures from the bottom of the tree to the top (the general indicator) was defined.

From the answers to the questionnaires, the quality indicators were then computed.

14.2.2.2 Results Analysis

For the analysis, several studies were performed:

- histograms of answers to the questions of the questionnaires;
- means and standard deviations of the number of answers per population, and of each indicator;
- histograms of the indicators, classified according to the transport sites, the interviewee profiles (populations), and the companies;
- main component analyses on the indicators;
- crossed analyses of questions;
- multiple correspondence analysis.

This work led to a definition of another way for computing the indicators by redefining the figures of merit assigned to the multiple-choice questions.

From these studies, the results for each indicator were analyzed and interpreted, as well as the connections between the indicators, and between the user and computing department staff answers.

14.3 Experience Gained

The experience gained from this measurement practice is summarized below.

14.3.1 Definition of Questionnaires

The questionnaires must be adapted to the type of people who will answer them. Each questionnaire should:

- be as short and as precise as possible;

- include only the questions related to the issues the interviewee is concerned with;

- include easily understandable words (for example, no technical words in an end-user questionnaire).

Another lesson is that an iterative method should be used to define the questionnaires; at least two cycles, separated by a real sampling test, are desirable.

14.3.2 Definition and Computation of Quality Indicators

The method that quality indicators are defined and computed can largely influence the resulting figures. The method should be precisely defined, and tested on real examples.

Moreover, the aggregation of indicators (for example through taking their mean) leads to the loss of some information. Thus, a low indicator can be neutralized by a high one, and then their mean is meaningless. This is the reason why the histograms of the answers were examined, as well as all the indicators (from the bottom to the top of the indicator trees).

This implies that the analysis must be performed at different levels. The highest levels only give a value to the general quality indicators, whereas the lowest levels enable analysis of the results, i.e., to find the issues which the interviewees judge weak, the relationships between these opinions, etc. These different analysis levels can be dedicated to different types of readers (e.g. top managers, technical managers).

14.3.3 Results Analysis

On the one hand, the statistical data analysis can only be performed if the number of interviewees is greater than one hundred.

On the other hand, the textual answers to questions should be specifically processed:

- if possible, the answers can be coded, and then handled as answers to multiple-choice questions;

- otherwise a textual data analysis tool should be used.

14.3.4 General Experience

The first general lesson learned is that there is a need to use tools to record the answers of the interviewees, and to perform the computations and the data analysis. In this case, a specific tool built using the Data Base Management System ORACLE and the spreadsheet LOTUS was developed, and the data analysis tool SPAD was used.

Lastly, this type of survey is not always suited to get any type of information. For example, the users were asked for their satisfaction concerning the training sessions which they had taken. In the event that they had taken several, it was not known whether their opinion applied to all sessions, to the last one, or whether they gave an averaged opinion. In this case, it would be better to design forms which could include questions similar to the ones in the questionnaires that the users would fill out at the end of each training session.

14.4 Conclusion

The measurement approach described here was judged positive by the computing department of the transport company. From the survey results, they decided to initiate some quality improvement actions. For example, they decided to put emphasis on the early phases of the software development life-cycle, especially the definition of the users' role during the requirements specification.

To follow-up on the results of these actions, it was decided that these surveys would be periodically conducted at least once per year.

15 Conclusions

15.1 Best Practices Summary

As described above, the approach for improving product quality and development team productivity using a Metrics Program is straightforward. Quality improvement goals are established which are derived from and supportive of the business objectives of the organization. Metrics are then defined which are used to measure progress against the goals. The metrics provide insights for identifying actions that can be implemented for improving the software development process. The metrics can then be used to provide feedback concerning the impact of the actions taken to improve the software development process. This closed-loop feedback mechanism approach is illustrated in Figure 15.1.

The summary of best practices described in this book is given in Table 15.1. Having observed the practices of these software development organizations, we can conclude that the use of metrics is a powerful tool for identifying actions to continually improve the software development process. The use of metrics is necessary to move software development from a 'craft' or 'art' to an engineering discipline consisting of a controlled, continually improved production process.

The activities described in this book represent a number of diverse software applications, environments, and development processes. The common elements which resulted in improvements in software quality and productivity are summarized as suggestions on using metrics for software project management. The techniques have all been applied within industrial organizations, and are thus practical methods which can be applied by others. The use of quantitative approaches to software management must be customized to the specific goals and development process of the particular organization. The metrics themselves are not important; rather it is the improved development process actions for which the metrics give insight that initiate quality and productivity improvement. The insights suggest improvements that either fill gaps or streamline the development process.

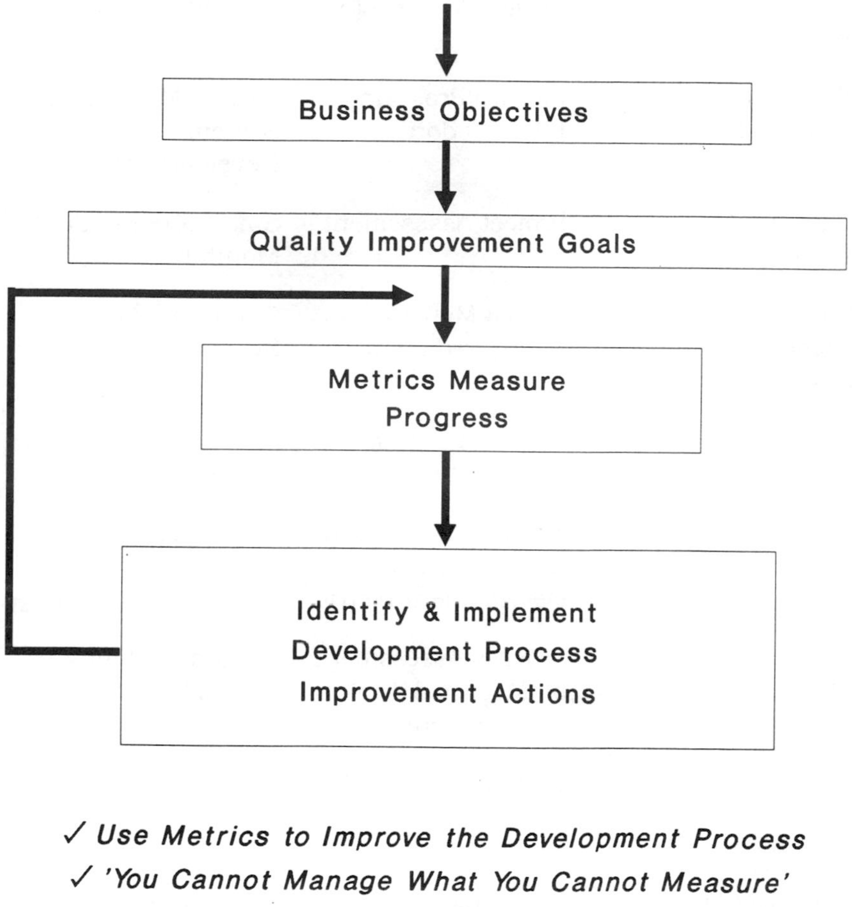

Figure 15.1 Metrics Program Approach.

Table 15.1 Best Practices Summary

Company	*Practice Area*	*Application*
Siemens Nixdorf Informationssysteme	Quality Metrics	Computer System Software Development and Maintenance
Siemens Nixdorf Informationssysteme	Subjective Metrics	Custom Application Software
Siemens Medical Electronics	Metrics Program Introduction	Patient Monitoring System Product Development
Siemens Medical Electronics	Project Assessment	Small Sized Patient Monitor
Siemens Private Communication Systems	Global Metrics, Fault Prediction	Communication Systems
Siemens Automation	Metrics Program Introduction	Factory Automation Systems
Data Logic	Process Assessment by Metrics & Project Development Metrics	Customer Projects
Data Logic	Process Assessment by Metrics & Project Development Metrics	Customer Billing System
Data Logic	Global Metrics	Networked PCs
Data Logic	Global Metrics	Manufacturing
ETNOTEAM	Maintenance Product Assessment	Consulting
ETNOTEAM	Quality System Introduction	Banking

VERIDATAS	Code Review Metrics	Software Purchasing
RW-TÜV	Test Coverage Metrics	Safety Critical Process Monitoring System
CRIL	Customer Satisfaction Measurement	Transportation Company

15.2 Benefits

Some of the Metrics Program benefits resulting from the best practices described in this book are summarized below.

- ***Improved Product Quality.*** The Metrics Program defines methods to measure product quality, and thus improvements resulting from actions taken can be observed from the metrics.

- ***Increased Development Team Productivity.*** The Metrics Program defines methods to measure software productivity, and thus improvements resulting from actions taken can be observed from the metrics.

- ***Better Project Planning and Estimation.*** When historical project metric data is available, comparisons can be made between new projects and similar prior projects. This improves the organization's ability to estimate costs and schedules for new projects such that better business decisions can be made.

- ***Better Project Management.*** The metric data provides project tracking such that corrective actions can be made to the project plan to increase the probability of successful completion of the project. The metric data is a communication vehicle between business management and software product development for helping to evaluate the status of projects and the quality levels of products prior to shipment to customers.

- ***Company Quality Culture.*** The Metrics Program, when used in conjunction with an overall quality and productivity improvement program, can beneficially contribute to achieving a company culture in which high quality products and development process are valued.

- ***Increased Customer Satisfaction.*** Software products containing fewer faults at time of shipment that are delivered on schedule will help increase customer satisfaction. In addition, customer confidence will increase in those vendors who demonstrate a commitment to improved product and development process quality.

- ***Increased Visibility of the Software Development Process.*** The Metrics Program provides visibility on the entire software development process, and it thus reduces its apparent complexity. This helps demystify software development by making it more understandable through its similarity to other industrial development processes.

15.3 Summary

As summarized by the collection of best practices contained in this book, the applications and development environments used by outstanding software organizations are very different. There are no firm answers or fixed rules for achieving excellence in software project management. The specific practices used are heavily dependent on the organizational culture and environment. Experimentation and flexibility are necessary for introducing improvements to the software development process. The suggestions given in this book do not guarantee a quick fix to the software problem. Rather the approach proposed consists of a number of incremental improvements which results in a better software development process over time. The use of metrics contributes significantly to a better understanding of which software development process improvements are desirable. Metrics also provide feedback on the effects of improvement actions that have been previously implemented.

It is hoped that the suggestions given in this book will stimulate increased application of software metrics to software project management. The key to improving software quality and productivity is by improving the process used to develop and maintain software products. The use of metrics is a proven technique for guiding the actions which are taken to improve the software development process. The metrics provide an indication of where improvements are most required, and they provide feedback on the effect of the actions taken. An improved software development process will result in better higher quality products that are developed with more productive resources within a shorter time schedule.

Appendix A. References

This Appendix provides an annotated list of references that were used in this book. In particular there are five textbooks which can be useful for the new practitioner of metrics. These include Boehm (1981) which provides comprehensive information on software estimation, life-cycle, and project management; Conte (1986) which provides a good collection of metrics definitions and functions; and Grady (1987) which describes metrics implementation experience at Hewlett-Packard. Two recent textbooks describe modern practices of software metrics in Europe (Fenton, 1991) and the USA (Jones, 1991).

Albrecht, A.J. (1979) Measuring Application Development Productivity. *Proc. of the Joint SHARE/GUIDE Symposium*, pp. 83-92.

This paper introduces the concept of Function Points for measuring software size. Its application is given for productivity measurement.

Albrecht, A.J. and Gaffney, J.E. (1983) Software Function, Source Lines of Code and Development Effort Prediction: A Software Science Validation. *IEEE Trans. on Software Engineering*, Vol. SE-9, No. 6, pp. 639-648.

This paper compares the use of function points with other methods for measuring software size.

Andersen, O. (1990) The Use of Software Engineering Data in Support of Project Management. *Software Engineering Journal*, Nov. 1990, pp. 350-356.

This paper is based on results of the ESPRIT REQUEST Project.

Arthur, J. (1984) Software Quality Measurements. *Datamation*, Dec. 1984.

This paper describes a quality model which is one of the ancestors of the ISO 9126 model.

Basili, V.R. (1979a) Quantitative Software Complexity Model: A Panel Summary. *Workshop on Quantitative Software Models for Reliability, Complexity, and Cost*, Oct. 1979.

Approaches to development metrics, and their use for software development are discussed.

Basili, V.R. and Reiter, R.W. (1979b) Evaluating Automatable Measures of Software Development. *Workshop on Quantitative Software Models for Reliability, Complexity, and Cost*, Oct. 1979.

Sample metrics are defined and evaluated in terms of ability to automate. Job steps, program size and changes, and graph cyclomatic complexity are tested in the context of disciplined programming methodology and teamwork.

Basili, V.R. (1980) Tutorial on Models and Metrics for Software Management and Engineering. IEEE Computer Society Press, Los Alamitos, CA.

Basili, V.R. and Weiss, D. (1984) A Methodology for Collecting Valid Software Engineering Data. *IEEE Trans. on Software Engineering*, Vol. SE-10, No. 3, Nov. 1984, pp. 728-738.

This paper introduces the GQM - Goals/Questions/Metrics - data collection and performance improvement approach.

Basili, V.R. and Rombach, H.D. (1991) Support for comprehensive reuse. *Software Engineering Journal*, Sep. 1991, pp. 303-316.

This paper defines models and support mechanisms for the reuse of software-related experience.

Beizer, B. (1984) *Software System Testing and Quality Assurance*. Van Nostrand Reinhold, New York.

This is an excellent book containing much practical advice for software testers.

Boehm, B.W. (1981) *Software Engineering Economics.* Prentice-Hall, Englewood Cliffs, NJ.

The COCOMO estimation model is described in detail. Statistics are used to refine metrics and estimation knowledge. This is a primary textbook on software estimation, and a technology driver for today's metrication techniques.

Brooks, F.P. (1982) *The Mythical Man-Month: Essays on Software Engineering.* Addison-Wesley, Reading, MA.

This book describes some of the management problems associated with large software projects based upon IBM OS/360 development experience.

Burrows, P. (1991) In Search of the Perfect Product. *Electronic Business*, June 17, 1991, pp. 70-74.

This paper provides a description of the application of Quality Function Deployment (QFD).

Card, D.N. and Glass, R.L. (1990) *Measuring Software Design Quality.* Prentice-Hall, Englewood Cliffs, NJ.

This book provides examples of software design metrics.

Carsana, L., Lancellotti, R., and Maiocchi, M. (1991) Software Metrics Measurement and Interpretation: Definition and Experimentation of a Flexible Technical Environment. *EUROMETRICS '91*, Mar. 1991, Paris, France.

Describes an environment for 'measurement by metrics'. Describes the integration of a code analyzer for measurement, and a spreadsheet for regression analysis and interpretation.

Cobb, R.H. and Mills, H.D. (1990) Engineering Software under Statistical Quality Control. *IEEE Software*, Nov. 1990, pp. 44-54.

This paper describes Cleanroom Software Engineering practices and metrics.

Computing Services Association Briefing Note (1990) Software Quality Metrics. Publ. No. 1.0, London, Nov. 1990.

This paper describes the Software Metrics Framework which is used extensively in this book.

Conte, S.D., Dunsmore, H.E., and Shen, V.Y. (1986) *Software Engineering Metrics and Models.* Benjamin/Cummings Publ. Co., Menlo Park, CA.

This book is a good collection of software metrics experience and information. It presents data concerning the relationships between the various metrics and program behavior.

Copigneaux, F. (1991) Trends Analysis in Software Metrication. *EUROMETRICS '91*, Mar. 1991, Paris, France.

This paper discusses direct and reverse McCall metrics, subjective metrics, and global metrics. It discusses the difficulty of relating low-level data to globally meaningful indicators.

Coté, V., Bourque, P., Oligny, S., and Rivard, N. (1988) Software Metrics: An Overview of Recent Results. *The Journal of Systems and Software*, **8**, pp. 121-131.

Cusumano, M.A. (1991) *Japan's Software Factories: A Challenge to U.S. Management.* Oxford University Press, New York.

This book contains an excellent description of the characteristics and evolution of the Japanese Software Factories at Hitachi, Toshiba, NEC, and Fujitsu.

Data Logic (1989) Project Metrics Procedure. Data Logic Corporate Standard, Ref. Q2314, Vs. 2.0, July 1989.

DeMarco, T. (1982) *Controlling Software Projects: Management, Measurement, & Estimation.* Yourdon Press, New York.

Presents a customizable methodology for using metrics.

Dreger, J.B. (1989) *Function Point Analysis.* Prentice-Hall, Englewood Cliffs, NJ.

This is a primary textbook for teaching Function Point Analysis.

Dumaine, B. (1989) How Managers Can Succeed Through Speed. *Fortune*, Feb. 13, 1989.

This paper identifies the benefits of applying Simultaneous Engineering techniques to the product development process. It identifies the business economics associated with early market introduction of the product. Due to the increased sales resulting from an early market introduction, it suggests higher development investment if the schedule can be reduced.

Fagan, M.E. (1976) Design and Code Inspections to Reduce Errors in Program Development. *IBM Systems Journal*, Vol. 15, No. 3, pp. 182-210.

This is the first paper describing the inspection technique which became known as 'Fagan' Inspections.

FDA (1989) Preproduction Quality Assurance Planning: Recommendations for Medical Device Manufacturers. Food and Drug Administration, Rockville, MD, Sep. 1989.

This document is a primary set of guidelines developed by the US FDA for the development of medical device software. Due to the safety critical requirements for these products, there is a strong emphasis on controlled development process for achieving high software product quality.

Feigenbaum, A.V. (1983) *Total Quality Control*. McGraw-Hill, New York.

This book describes the TQM process.

Fenton, N.E. (1991) *Software Metrics, A Rigorous Approach*, Chapman & Hall, London.

Provides a framework for software measurement. Includes material developed for the ESPRIT METKIT Project.

Gaffney, J.E. (1981) Metrics in Software Quality Assurance. Tutorial abstract - *ACM '81*, Nov. 9-11, 1981, pp. 126-130.

This is an early tutorial paper on the application of quantitative methods for improving software quality. The material was originally presented at a tutorial at the ACM SIGMETRICS Workshop/Symposium on Measurement and Evaluation of Software Quality on March 25, 1981.

Gill, G.K. and Kemerer, C.F. (1991) Cyclomatic Complexity Density and Software Maintenance Productivity. *IEEE Trans. on SW Engr.*, Vol. 17, No. 12, Dec. 1991, pp. 1284-1288.

This paper describes the relationship between software maintenance productivity and McCabe's cyclomatic complexity measure.

Gordon, F. and Isenhour, R. (1989) Simultaneous Engineering. *Engineering Manager*, Jan. 30, 1989.

The principles of concurrent product development are discussed.

Grady, R.B. and Caswell, D.L. (1987) *Software Metrics: Establishing a Company-Wide Program.* Prentice-Hall, Englewood Cliffs, NJ.

A very good presentation of a 'Management by Metrics' approach in an industrial environment. The book presents the experience of HP.

Halstead, M.H. (1977) *Elements of Software Science.* Elsevier, New York.

Contains all Halstead's equations and formulas, with derivations and experimental evidence.

Halstead, M.H. (1979) Advances in Software Science. *Advances in Computers.* Vol. 18, Academic Press, New York.

Hetzel, B. and Craig, R. (1990) Software Measures and Practices Benchmark Study. Research Reports TR900-904, Software Quality Engineering, Dec. 20, 1990, Jacksonville, FL.

These research reports contain the results of the industry study performed on software metrics and development practices.

Humphrey, W.S. and Sweet, W.L. (1987) A Method for Assessing the Software Engineering Capability of Contractors. Technical Report CMU/SEI-87-TR-23, Sep. 1987 - SEI, Pittsburgh, PA.

This presents the principles of Software Production Quality Systems, classifies them into five 'maturity levels', and provides guidelines for assessing a software process.

Humphrey, W.S. (1989) *Managing the Software Process.* Addison-Wesley, Reading, MA.

This book describes the SEI Process Maturity Model.

Humphrey, W.S. (1991) Software and the factory paradigm. *Software Engineering Journal,* Sep. 1991, pp. 370-376.

This paper describes approaches to continuous software process improvement.

IEEE (1987) Software Engineering Standards. ISBN 471-63457-3.

This is a set of standards for controlling the Software Engineering Process.

IEEE (1989) Standard Glossary of Software Engineering Terminology. P610.12, Mar. 30, 1990.

This document contains a list of definitions for commonly used software engineering terms.

IEEE (1990a) Draft Standard for a Software Quality Metrics Methodology. P-1061/D21, Apr. 1, 1990.

Currently undergoing review and revision.

IEEE (1990b) Standard for Software Productivity Metrics. P-1045/D3.1, Aug. 28, 1990.

This standard contains definitions of metrics used for calculating productivity such as source code, function points, document size, and effort.

IFPUG (1990) Function Point Counting Practices Manual. International Function Point Users Group.

This manual describes standard methods for counting function points.

ISO (1990) ISO/DIS 9000-3 - Quality Management and Quality Assurance Standards - Part 3: Guidelines for the Application of ISO 9001 to the Development, Supply and Maintenance of Software. Sep. 1990.

This describes software development environment requirements in order to be compliant with the ISO 9001 standard. It examines requirements on technical activities (development phases), management activities (configuration control, purchasing, etc.), and quality system evolution.

Jones, T.C. (1978) Measuring Programming Quality and Productivity. *IBM System Journal*, Vol. 17, No. 1.

Estimation technique is discussed including possible erroneous interpretations in software measurement.

Jones, T.C. (1991) *Applied Software Measurement*. McGraw-Hill, New York.

This book describes current measurement practices for software organizations in U.S. companies.

Kitchenham, B.A. and McDermid, J.A. (1986) Software Metrics and Integrated Project Support Environments. *Software Engineering Journal*, Jan. 1986, pp. 58-64.

Lautenbach (1990) *IBM Horizons*, Quality Special Edition, IBM US, Feb. 1990.

This newspaper describes the goals of IBM US for achieving improved quality over the next five years.

Madhavji, N.H. (1991) The process cycle. *Software Engineering Journal*, Sep. 1991, pp. 234-242.

This paper describes the discipline of software process engineering which includes software development process understanding and support.

Maiocchi, M., Mazzetti, A., Oliva, M., and Villa, M. (1984) TEFAX: An Automated Test Factory for Functional Quality Control of Software Projects. *Colloque de génie logiciel 2* - Nice.

A method for extracting information for functional coverage of software testing is presented, along with a tool supporting it.

Maiocchi, M. (1990a) Automatic Software Validation as a Key Towards Quality at Low Cost. *5th NATO Symposium on Quality and its Assurance*, Madrid, June 1990.

The advantages and philosophy of the automation of generation of software tests is presented and discussed.

Maiocchi, M. (1990b) Software Engineering. *Symposium on Emerging Information Technologies*, EIT, Amsterdam, Dec. 1990.

The role of software engineering is presented with respect to the relevance of organization and CASE tools.

Maiocchi, M. (1990c) Software Quality: Models, Techniques, Assurance, Certification. *ISATA Conference*, Florence.

A software quality model is presented. Beginning with the requirements, the quality attributes, technical attributes, technical documents, measures, and the V&V plan are derived for embedded real-time systems.

Matsubara, T. (1991) Project Management in Japan. *American Programmer*, Vol. 4, No. 6, June 1991, pp. 41-50.

This paper describes some software project management practices at Hitachi Software.

Mayrhauser, A. (1990) *Software Engineering: Methods and Management*. Academic Press, New York.

This is a large, complete, and up-to-date presentation of software engineering methods and management issues.

Mays, R.G., Jones, C.L., Halloway, G.J., and Studinski, D.P. (1990) Experiences with Defect Prevention. *IBM Systems Journal*, Vol. 29, No. 1, pp. 4-32.

This paper describes IBM's experience with a Software Defect Prevention Process.

McCabe, T.J. (1976) A Complexity Measure. *IEEE Trans. on SW Eng.*, Vol. 2, No. 4, Dec. 1976.

This is the initial paper on cyclomatic complexity definition.

McCall, J.A. (1980) An Assessment of Current Software Metric Research. *EASCON'80.*

Graphs representing program control flow are compared to program complexity.

Möller, K.H. (1988) Increasing of Software Quality by Objectives and Residual Fault Prognosis. *First European Seminar on Software Quality*, Apr. 1988.

Discusses the approach for improving software quality through metrics data collection in the area of fault-counting at various phases of the software development process.

Möller, K.H. (1991) Qualitätsmetrik Software. Proposed SIEMENS Metrics System Standard.

Musa, J.D. (1980a) Software Reliability Measurement. *The Journal of Systems and Software*, Vol. 1, No. 3.

A model of software reliability based upon execution time of programs is developed. Execution (CPU) time is then related to project calendar time.

Musa, J.D. (1980b) The Measurement and Management of Software Reliability. *Proc. IEEE*, Vol. 68, No. 9, Sep. 1980.

Contains details of Musa's and Littlewood's reliability theories.

Musa, J.D., Iannino, A., and Okumoto, K. (1987) *Software Reliability: Measurement, Prediction, Application.* McGraw-Hill, New York.

This is a comprehensive reference book on software reliability and measurements.

NATO (1987) AQAP-13 - NATO Software Control System Requirements. Aug. 1987.

Describes the requirements for a software development environment for producing high quality software.

Navlakha, J. (1986) Software Productivity Metrics: Some Candidates and Their Evaluation. *National Computer Conference* 1986, pp. 69-75.

Paulish, D.J. (1990a) Methods & Metrics for Developing High Quality Patient Monitoring System Software. *Proc. of the Third IEEE Symposium on Computer-Based Medical Systems*, Chapel Hill, NC, June 1990, pp. 145-152.

This paper describes the experience of implementing a Metrics Program at Siemens Medical Electronics, Inc.

Paulish, D.J. (1990b) Methods & Metrics for Improving the Functional Testing of Patient Monitoring System Software. *Proc. of the Seventh International Conference on Testing Computer Software*, San Francisco, June 1990, pp. 119-127.

This paper describes experience with applying metrics to independent software validation testing.

Putnam, L. (1980) Tutorial on Software Cost Estimating and Life Cycle Control: Getting the Software Numbers. Computer Society Press, Los Alamitos, CA.

This tutorial consists of several papers describing various estimation models and techniques.

Putnam, L. (1991) Trends in Measurement, Estimation, and Control. *IEEE Software*, Mar. 1991, pp. 105-107.

Provides current trends in software metrics including example basic metrics.

Royce, W.W. (1970) Managing the Development of Large Software Systems: Concepts and Techniques. *WESCON Conference Proceedings*, Aug. 1970.

This paper presents an early life-cycle model for the software development process.

Schlender, B.R. (1989) How to Break the Software Logjam. *Fortune*

Magazine, Sep. 1989, pp. 108-112.

Gives a number of examples of software projects and the difficulty with managing them. Provides some suggestions on how to improve the software development production process.

Schmelzer, H.J. (1989) How to Gain a Competitive Edge. *SIEMENS Review*, Nov./Dec. 1989, vol. 56, 6/89.

Describes the application of techniques to the product development process for reducing the time it takes to develop new products.

SEI (1991) Capability Maturity Model for Software. Tech. Report CMU/SEI-91-TR-24.

This report outlines an updated SEI Process Maturity Model.

Selby, R.W., Basili, V.R., and Baker, F.T. (1987) Cleanroom Software Development: An Empirical Evaluation. *IEEE Trans. SW Engr.*, Sep. 1987, pp. 1027-1037.

This paper analyzes the performance of software engineers using Cleanroom Engineering practices.

Sherer, S.A. (1991) A Cost-Effective Approach to Testing. *IEEE Software*, Mar. 1991, pp. 34-40.

Provides an approach to determine when the consequences of a software failure no longer justify the testing cost.

Appendix B. Glossary of Acronyms

ADC	Application Development Center
ANSI	American National Standards Institute
ASCII	American Standard Code for Information Interchange
AT&T	American Telephone & Telegraph
ATC	Athens Technology Center
BC	Business (Financial) Controller
BCS	British Computer Society
BSD	Business Systems Definition
CASE	Computer-Aided Software Engineering
CIM	Computer-Integrated Manufacturing
COCOMO	Constructive Cost Model
COSMOS	Cost Management with Metrics of Specification
CPU	Central Processing Unit
CSA	Computing Services Association
DDC	Development Document Control
DEMETER	Design Metrics Evaluator
DLOC	Delta Lines of Code

DM	Deutsche Mark
DOS	Disk Operating System
DRM	Defect Removal Model
ECO	Engineering Change Order
EDP	Electronic Data Processing
EKG (ECG)	Electrocardiogram
ESPRIT	European Strategic Programme for Research and Development in Information Technology
FDA	Food & Drug Administration
G/Q/M	Goals/Questions/Metrics
HP	Hewlett-Packard
HW	Hardware
IBM	International Business Machines
IEEE	Institute of Electrical and Electronics Engineers
ISDN	Integrated Services Data Network
ISO	International Standards Organization
IT	Information Technology
KPR	Known Problem Report
LAN	Local Area Network
LOC	Lines of Code
MERMAID	Metrication and Resource Modeling Aid
METKIT	Metrics Education Toolkit
MR	Modification Request
MTBF	Mean-Time-Between-Failures
MTTF	Mean-Time-To-Failure

MUSE	Metrics Use in Software Engineering (for Quality and Reliability)
NASA	National Aeronautics and Space Administration
NCR	National Cash Register
NLOC	Net Lines of Code
OCD	Organization and Computing Department
PBX	Private Branch Exchange
PC	Personal Computer
PCG	Product Control Group
PCS	Project Control System
PMW	Project Manager Workbench
PPP	Product Planning Process
PROLOC	Program Lines of Code
PROM	Programmable Read-Only Memory
QA	Quality Assurance
QFD	Quality Function Deployment
QM	Quality Management
R&D	Research & Development
REQUEST	Reliability and Quality of European Software
SCCS	Source Code Control System
SCOPE	Software Certification on Program in Europe
SDLC	Systems Development Life-Cycle
SDR	System Difficulty Report
SEI	Software Engineering Institute
SEL	Software Engineering Laboratory

SME	Siemens Medical Electronics
SNI	Siemens Nixdorf Informationssysteme
SPEM	Software Productivity Evaluation Model
SPL	Systems Programming Language
SPR	Software Problem Report
SPR	Software Productivity Research, Inc.
SQE	Software Quality Engineering
SVR	System Variation Request
SW	Software
TC	Technical Controller
TQM	Total Quality Management
V&V	Verification & Validation

Index